A VERY BAD WIZARD

MORALITY BEHIND THE CURTAIN

by

TAMLER SOMMERS

BELIEVER BOOKS

a division of
McSWEENEY'S

BELIEVER BOOKS

a division of
McSWEENEY'S

Copyright © 2009 McSweeney's, the *Believer,* and Tamler Sommers

Several of these interviews previously appeared in the *Believer.*
www.believermag.com

Cover design by Brian McMullen. Cover art by Charles Burns.

Printed in Canada by Westcan Printing Group

ISBN: 978-1-934781-38-8

CONTENTS

To Jen and Eliza

A
VERY
BAD
WIZARD

INTRODUCTION

QUESTIONS FOR THE INTERVIEWER

Why interviews? Don't philosophers write articles and books?

Yes, and that's a good thing. But the interview format has its advantages too. In books and articles, the arguments are worked out beforehand and then presented to the reader in digested form. Interviews allow for the ideas to be challenged and developed during the piece itself—and that's exciting stuff for a philosopher. There's a reason Plato only wrote dialogues. Questions, objections, responses to objections—these are the things that make philosophy move forward. But even in philosophical dialogues the authors know where the debate is heading. Dialogues are constructed to reach conclusions arrived at beforehand. I was able to ask questions without knowing what the answers would be. I never knew what direction the interview would take until it was happening. Like I said, exciting stuff for a philosopher.

What's up with the title?

The title refers to a scene at the end of *The Wizard of Oz,* when Dorothy and friends return to the Wizard's palace to claim their reward after making short work of the Wicked Witch of the West.

The Wizard—in the form of an enormous floating green head—stalls, telling them to come back the next day. The group starts to protest and the green head fulminates about the dangers of arousing the wrath of the Wizard. Meanwhile, little Toto runs off to a booth by the side of the hall and pulls back a curtain to reveal that the Great and Powerful Oz is really just a balding carnival barker from Kansas. The green head, explosions, fire, and smoke are mere illusions produced by a machine. Dorothy is outraged.

"You're a very bad man!" she tells him.

"Oh no, my dear," the Wizard replies, "I'm a very good man. I'm just a very bad wizard."

And he is a good man. Because now that the illusion has been exposed, the Wizard can show our heroes that they've spent the movie searching for something they already have. The Scarecrow's brain, the Tin Man's heart, the Lion's courage, and Dorothy's ability to return home have been inside them all along… naturally. Wizardry not required. I think the same is true for all of us when it comes to morality. We don't need a lot of smoke and mirrors, we don't need illusions. We have what we need, naturally.

So the guiding figure of this book is a cairn terrier?

Hey, Toto does what every philosopher and scientist tries to do: he uncovers the truth about how something in the world actually works. As a philosopher, my aim is to understand the kind of morality and freedom we really have, not the kind we want to have. And I've been drawn to work in other disciplines that can shed light on this question. This book has allowed me to go straight to the source, to talk with the researchers who are using technology and scientific techniques never before available to make thrilling advances in the science of human nature. The goal of every interview is to pull back part of the curtain that conceals the inner workings of our moral lives.

Isn't that a little dangerous?

It's true that some people feel threatened by the prospect of naturalizing morality. They think morality has been underwritten by God, or some equally mysterious understanding of Reason with a capital *R*. Science, they worry, may reveal ethics to be a sham. I think this fear is misguided, as misguided as the Tin Man's belief that his heart couldn't be made of tin. Learning what makes a car run doesn't stop it from running. Morality is out there— what could be more exciting than discovering the true origins and mechanisms that lie beneath it? We shouldn't be scared about what we'll find. All we need to do is…

… follow the yellow brick road?

You said it, not me.

A NOTE ABOUT
THE INTERVIEWS

Interviews are grouped by theme into three parts. Each part begins with a brief introduction, and each interview begins with a detailed introduction covering the subject and his or her work.

The interviews with Galen Strawson, Michael Ruse, Jonathan Haidt, Frans de Waal, and Philip Zimbardo previously appeared in the *Believer.* I have left the original introductions for these interviews intact.

PART ONE

HOW FREE ARE WE?

Samuel Johnson once remarked that "all theory is against the freedom of the will; all experience is for it." For thousands of years, philosophers and scientists have mounted strong theoretical arguments against free will, and for thousands of years people have remained unconvinced. Why? Because we *feel* free. We *feel* responsible. That may be true, but it also feels like the earth is flat, stationary, and at the center of the solar system. In almost every other field we allow logic and science to trump experience—why not here?

One reason is that the ethical implications of denying free will and moral responsibility seem dreadful. We fear it would void our lives of meaning and purpose, and perhaps lead to a world where "everything is permitted" and no one is held accountable for anything. If free will is an illusion, is it one we're better off embracing?

Not according to the authors interviewed in this section. In Chapter 1, the philosopher Galen Strawson argues that we cannot freely create our characters, and therefore are not ultimately responsible for our behavior. Nevertheless, according to Strawson, a life without free will can be a fulfilling one. In Chapter 2, Philip Zimbardo discusses various studies (including his own) that suggest that our characters are far less stable than we think. Situational elements—our immediate social and physical environment—exert tremendous influence over our behavior. According to Zimbardo, pulling back the curtain to reveal the true causes of our behavior will lead to a more just and effective approach to education, foreign policy, and criminal justice.

1

GALEN STRAWSON

"YOU CANNOT MAKE YOURSELF THE WAY YOU ARE."

"You sound to me as though you don't believe in free will," said Billy Pilgrim.

"If I hadn't spent so much time studying Earthlings," said the Tralfamadorian, "I wouldn't have any idea what was meant by 'free will.' I've visited thirty-one inhabited planets in the universe, and I have studied reports on one hundred more. Only on Earth is there any talk of free will."

— Kurt Vonnegut, *Slaughterhouse-Five*

Imagine for a moment that it was not Timothy McVeigh who destroyed the Alfred P. Murrah Federal Building in Oklahoma City, but a mouse. Suppose this mouse got into the wiring of the electrical system, tangled the circuits, and caused a big fire, killing all those inside. Now think of the victims' families. There would, of course, still be enormous grief and suffering, but there would be one significant difference: there would be no resentment, no consuming anger, no hatred, no need to see the perpetrator punished (even if the mouse somehow got out of the building) in order to experience "closure." Why the difference? Because McVeigh, we think, committed this terrible act of his own free will. He chose to do it, and he could have chosen not to. McVeigh, then, is morally responsible for the death of the victims in a way that the mouse would not be. And our sense of justice demands that he pay for this crime.

Humans have an undeniable tendency to see ourselves as free and morally responsible beings. But there's a problem. We also believe—most of us, anyhow—that our environment and our heredity entirely shape our characters. (What else could?) But we aren't responsible for our environment, and we aren't responsible for our heredity. So we aren't responsible for our characters. But then how can we be responsible for acts that arise from our characters?

There's a simple but extremely unpopular answer to this question: we aren't. We are not and cannot be ultimately responsible for our behavior. According to this view, while it may be of great pragmatic value to hold people responsible for their actions, and to employ systems of reward and punishment, no one is really deserving of blame or praise for anything. This answer has been around for more than two thousand years; it is backed by solid arguments with premises that are consistent with how most of us view the world. Yet few today give this position the serious consideration it deserves. The view that free will is a fiction is called counterintuitive, absurd, pessimistic, pernicious, and, most commonly, unacceptable, even by those who recognize the force of the arguments behind it. Philosophers who reject God, an immaterial soul, and even absolute morality, cannot bring themselves to do the same for the concept of free will—not in their day-to-day lives, but in books and articles and extraordinarily complex theories.

There are a few exceptions, however, and one of them is Galen Strawson, professor of philosophy at the University of Reading. Strawson is one of the most respected theorists in the free-will industry and, at the same time, a bit of an outsider. The two main philosophical camps engage in a technical and often bitter dispute over whether free will is compatible with the truth of determinism (the theory that the future is fixed, because every event has a cause, and the causes stretch back until the beginning of the universe). But if there is one thing that both sides agree on, it's that we do have free will and that we are morally responsible. Strawson, with a simple, powerful argument that we will discuss below, bets the other way.

Strawson's was not always such a minority view. Enlightenment philosophers like Spinoza, Diderot, Voltaire, and d'Holbach challenged ordinary conceptions of freedom, doubted whether we could be morally responsible, and looked to ground theories of blame and punishment in other ways. Strawson is a descendant of these philosophers, but still incorporates the British analytic tradition into his work. His views are clear and honest, and there are no cop-outs—quite unusual in a literature mired in obscure terminology and wishful thinking. And his essays are always deeply connected to everyday experience. One of the main issues Strawson addresses is why we so instinctively and stubbornly see ourselves as free and responsible. What is it about human experience that makes it difficult, maybe impossible, to believe something that we can easily demonstrate as true?

Galen Strawson is also the son of perhaps the most respected analytic philosopher of the past century, the great metaphysician and philosopher of language, P. F. Strawson.[1] Though not primarily concerned with the topic of free will, P. F. Strawson wrote one of the classic papers of the genre, an essay called "Freedom and Resentment." Galen (not from oedipal motives, he assures us) is one of its most effective critics.

March 2003

I. THE BUCK STOPS—WHERE?

TAMLER SOMMERS: You start out your book *Freedom and Belief* by saying that there is no such thing as free will. What exactly do you mean by "free will"?

---

[1] P. F. Strawson passed away in 2006.

GALEN STRAWSON: I mean what nearly everyone means. Almost all human beings believe that they are free to choose what to do in such a way that they can be truly, genuinely responsible for their actions in the strongest possible sense—responsible period, responsible without any qualification, responsible *sans phrase*, responsible *tout court*, absolutely, radically, buck-stoppingly responsible; *ultimately* responsible, in a word—and so ultimately *morally* responsible when moral matters are at issue. Free will is the thing you have to have if you're going to be responsible in this all-or-nothing way. That's what I mean by free will. That's what I think we haven't got and can't have.

I like philosophers—I love what they do; I love what I do—but they have made a truly unbelievable hash of all this. They've tried to make the phrase "free will" mean all sorts of different things, and each of them has told us that what it *really* means is what he or she has decided it *should* mean. But they haven't made the slightest impact on what it really means, or on our old, deep conviction that free will is something we have.

TS: That's true. Biologists, cognitive scientists, neurologists—they all seem to have an easier time, at least considering the possibility that there's no free will. But philosophers defend the concept against all odds, at the risk of terrible inconsistency with the rest of their views about the world. If it's a fact that there's no free will, why do philosophers have such a hard time accepting it?

GS: There's a Very Large Question here, as Winnie the Pooh would say. There's a question about the pathology of philosophy, or more generally about the weird psychological mechanisms that underwrite commitment to treasured beliefs—religious, theoretical, or whatever—in the face of overwhelming contrary evidence. But to be honest, I can't really accept it myself, and not because I'm a philosopher. As a philosopher I think the impossibility of free will and ultimate moral responsibility can be proved with complete certainty. It's just that I can't really live with this fact from day to day. Can you, really? As for the scientists, they may accept it in their white coats, but I'm sure they're just like the rest of us when they're out in the world—convinced of the reality of radical free will.

TS: Well, let's move on to the argument then. There's a famous saying of Schopenhauer's that goes like this: "A man can surely do what he wants to do. But he cannot determine what he wants." Is this idea at the core of your argument against moral responsibility?

GS: Yes—and it's an old thought. It's in Hobbes somewhere, and it's in Book Two of Locke's *Essay Concerning Human Understanding*, and I bet some ancient Greek said it, since they said almost everything.

Actually, though, there's a way in which it's not quite true. If you want to acquire some want or preference you haven't got, you can sometimes do so. You can cultivate it. Perhaps you're lazy and unfit and you want to acquire a love of exercise. Well, you can force yourself to do it every day and hope you come to like it. And you just might; you might even get addicted. Maybe you can do the same if you dislike olives.

TS: But then where did *that* desire come from—the desire to acquire the love of exercise... or olives?

GS: Right—now the deeper point cuts in. For suppose you do want to acquire a want you haven't got. The question is, where did the first want—the want for a want—come from? It seems it was just there, just a given, not something you chose or engineered. It was just there, like most of your preferences in food, music, footwear, sex, interior lighting, and so on.

I suppose it's possible that you might have acquired the first want, that's the want for a want, because you wanted to! It's *theoretically* possible that you had a want to have a want to have a want. But this is very hard to imagine, and the question just rearises: Where did *that* want come from? You certainly can't go on like this forever. At some point your wants must be just given. They will be products of your genetic inheritance and upbringing, in which you had no say. In other words, there's a fundamental sense in which you did not and cannot make yourself the way you are. And this, as you say, is the key step in the basic argument against ultimate moral responsibility, which goes like this:

(*1*) You do what you do—in the circumstances in which you find yourself—because of the way you are; (*2*) so if you're going to be ultimately responsible for what you do, you're going to have to be ultimately responsible for the way you are—at least in certain mental respects; (*3*) but you can't be ultimately responsible for the way you are (for the reasons just given); (*4*) so you can't be ultimately responsible for what you do.

TS: I suppose it's the third step that people have the most trouble accepting.

GS: Yes, although the step seems fairly clear when you look at it the right way. Sometimes people explain why (*3*) is true by saying that you can't be *causa sui*—you can't be the cause of yourself, you can't be truly or ultimately self-made in any way. As Nietzsche puts it, in his usual, tactful way:

> The *causa sui* is the best self-contradiction that has been conceived so far; it is a sort of rape and perversion of logic. But the extravagant pride of man has managed to entangle itself profoundly and frightfully with just this nonsense. The desire for "freedom of the will" in the superlative metaphysical sense, which still holds sway, unfortunately, in the minds of the half-educated; the desire to bear the entire and ultimate responsibility for one's actions oneself, and to absolve God, the world, ancestors, chance, and society involves nothing less than to be precisely this *causa sui* and, with more than Baron Münchhausen's audacity, to pull oneself up into existence by the hair, out of the swamps of nothingness.

There's lots more to say about this basic argument, and there are lots of ways in which people have tried to get around the conclusion. But none of them work.

II. VIEWING HITLER LIKE
THE LISBON EARTHQUAKE.

TS: I notice that the argument makes no mention of the theory of determinism. But historically the debate over freedom and responsibility has revolved around the truth of determinism, and the question of whether free will and moral responsibility are compatible with it.

GS: Yes, many people think that determinism—the view that the history of the universe is fixed, the view that everything that happens is strictly necessitated by what has already gone before, in such a way that nothing can ever happen otherwise than it does—is the real threat to free will, to ultimate moral responsibility. But the basic argument against ultimate moral responsibility works whether determinism is true or false. It's a completely a priori argument, as philosophers like to say. That means that you can see that it is true just lying on your couch. You don't have to get up off your couch and go outside and examine the way things are in the physical world. You don't have to do any science. And actually, current science isn't going to help. Ultimate moral responsibility is also ruled out by the theory of relativity. Einstein himself, in a piece written as a homage to the Indian mystical poet Rabindranath Tagore, said that "a Being, endowed with higher insight and more perfect intelligence, watching man and his doings, [would] smile about man's illusion that he was acting according to his own free will."

TS: And the illusion that he and others were morally responsible for their actions?

GS: Yes, but I just want to stress the word "ultimate" before "moral responsibility." Because there's a clearly weaker, everyday sense of "morally responsible" in which you and I and millions of other people are thoroughly morally responsible people.

TS: I suppose your lazy unfit man who acquires a love for exercise is responsible for his choice in this weaker everyday sense. He made the choice, and he acted on it. On the other hand, it seems that in order for this man to be *deserving of praise* for his decision, he would have to be morally responsible in the deeper sense, in the ultimate sense. And in fact, isn't that an implication of your argument—that no one is truly deserving of blame or praise for anything?

GS: Well, *truly* is a flexible word—again I think *ultimately* is better—but yes: no one can be ultimately deserving of praise or blame for anything. It's not possible. This is very, very hard to swallow, but that's how it is. Ultimately, it all comes down to luck: luck—good or bad—in being born the way we are, luck—good or bad—in what then happens to shape us. We can't be ultimately responsible for how we are in such a way as to have absolute, buck-stopping responsibility for what we do. At the same time, it seems we can't help believing that we do have absolute buck-stopping responsibility.

TS: You're right that many people find this hard to swallow. As you write in one of your essays, if it all comes down to luck, "even Hitler is let off the hook." So how should we regard Hitler and Stalin and other villains of history? Should we view them like we view the Lisbon earthquake, or the Plague?

GS: In the end, and in a sense: yes. Obviously it's wildly hard to accept. For some people I think it's impossible to accept, given their temperaments (they might not be able to make sense of their lives anymore). As I said, I can't really accept it myself—I can't live it all the time. If someone harmed or tortured or killed one of my children, I'd feel everything almost anyone else would feel. I'd probably have intense feelings of revenge. But these feelings would fade. In the end, they're small and self-concerned. Only the grief would last.

Maybe one way to put it is this: people in themselves aren't evil, there's no such thing as moral evil in that sense, but evil exists, great evil, and people can be carriers of great evil. You might reply, Look, if they're carriers of evil they just are evil, face the facts. But I would have to say that your response is, in the end, superficial. After all, we don't call natural disasters evil.

There's another thing to say about the Hitler case. Our sense that he must be held utterly responsible for what he did is both cognitive and emotional, and it usually seems to us that these two factors can't possibly come apart. The cognitive part, the sense that it is just an absolute objective fact that he is wholly responsible in the strongest possible way, seems inseparable from the noncognitive part, the moral nausea, the disgust, the anger, I don't know what to call it. They seem inseparable in the way that blood is inseparable from a living body (that was Shylock's problem). And since the non-cognitive emotional part is plainly a completely appropriate reaction it can seem that the cognitive part must be, too.

Nevertheless, I think they can come apart. Many of our emotional responses can stay in place when we confront the fact that there is no ultimate moral responsibility. We don't stop retching involuntarily when we realize that there is nothing objectively disgusting about a smell of decay. No doubt some of our emotional responses are *essentially* connected to belief in ultimate moral responsibility. But I think even the most emotionally intense desires for revenge and retribution, say, can be felt in a way that does not presuppose ultimate moral responsibility.

TS: I don't know. Take the case of Timothy McVeigh—his execution was shown to the families of the victims on closed-circuit TV. Why? So that the families could experience "closure." Don't you think that kind of retributive impulse presupposes a belief in moral responsibility? If a malfunctioning computer, or a mouse, had caused the death of their loved ones, would they have had to watch the destruction of the mouse (or computer) in order to attain this closure?

GS: What you say sounds right, so what can I say in reply? It's not enough for me to say that a hated human is just not the same as a hated mouse or computer. Quite so, you'll say, and that's precisely because we take a human to have ultimate moral responsibility. I'm sorry about repeating "ultimate" every time, but I think it's important. Let's just call it deep moral responsibility from now on, DMR for short. (It sounds like some exotic psychotropic drug.)

So I guess you're right. These desires for revenge and retribution are just not going to be the normal human thing if they don't involve the belief that the hated person has DMR. They're going to be unusual. So why did I say what I said? Partly because I was thinking of a remarkable book called *Revenge,* by Laura Blumenfeld, in which she describes cultures in which the whole business of revenge and vendetta gets ritualized. I don't think the Mafia has to believe in DMR to feel intense desires for revenge and retribution. And desire for retaliation doesn't require anything of the sort.

Which reminds me of something interesting: the old rule, older than the Old Testament, that says "Life for life, eye for eye, tooth for tooth, hand for hand, foot for foot, burning for burning, wound for wound, stripe for stripe" is almost universally misunderstood. It's not an intrinsically vengeful idea. It was intended as a counsel of restraint, of moderation in retaliation. Take an eye for an eye, it says, but no more. Measure for measure. No escalation. At one point Blumenfeld goes to the Roman Catholic region in northern Albania and asks a member of the local "Blood Feud Committee" about turning the other cheek. The guy just laughs—they all do, in the room, they titter—and says "In Albania we have 'Don't hit my cheek or I'll kill you.'" One feels they really got the hang of Christianity.

TS: So in your view, then, the idea of retaliation can play an important pragmatic role, but actual *belief* in deep moral responsibility isn't necessary to function as a human being.

GS: Not only isn't it necessary, it may even be harmful. I like what the psychologist Eleanor Rosch said in a talk she gave in San Francisco last August called "What Buddhist Meditation has to Tell Psychology about the Mind." At one point she was discussing the Buddhist doctrine of the endlessly ramifying interdependence of everything, and observed that "an understanding of [this] interdependence has clinical significance. It can provide people who suffer from guilt, depression, or anxiety with a vision of themselves as part of an interdependent network in which they need neither blame themselves nor feel powerless. In fact it may be that it is only when people are able to see the way in which they are not responsible for events that they can find the deeper level at which it is possible to take responsibility beyond concept and (depending upon the terminology of one's religious affiliation) repent, forgive, relax, or have power over the phenomenal world."

Trouble is, this is very, very hard to do. And it needs some explaining. Seeing the way in which you are not responsible for events in the manner that Eleanor Rosch describes certainly doesn't mean that you become an irresponsible person. Also, while some of us are fiercely self-critical, and would do well to ease up on ourselves—for self-criticism is another form of self-indulgence—we don't particularly want Hitler & Co. to "relax." It takes reflection to see the truth in what Eleanor Rosch is saying.

TS: Buddhist meditation and Buddhist philosophy in general appears in much of your work. Do you practice some form of meditation yourself?

GS: I tried meditation when I was an undergraduate (and putative flower-child, with hair to my waist) at Cambridge in the UK in the late 1960s and early 1970s, but I've never managed to keep it up.... I tried again last year, after a twenty-five year gap, using Patricia Carrington's utterly dogma-free method of "clinically standardized meditation." It was pretty interesting, but I lapsed again.

TS: Did you feel, when you were doing it, that meditating made the denial of free will and DMR easier to accept—I mean on more than just a theoretical level?

GS: Well, the denial of DMR didn't come to mind when I was actually meditating, or trying to, though I think it would have seemed pretty natural if it had. But perhaps you're asking whether meditation made a discernible difference to my attitude to DMR in the rest of my daily life. The answer is that I don't think so, though it might well have done so if I'd been better about it, or gone on for longer.

So can I live the denial of free will and DMR rather than just accept it theoretically? Well, if I think I've done something bad, I feel wholly responsible—I feel remorse, regret, and so on. So, no. But perhaps the remorse doesn't endure for too long. I think that if such feelings persist too long, they become self-indulgent in some deep way. I think, in fact, that all guilt is self-indulgent—it's all about self—while things like remorse and contrition are not, although they can become so if they get ritualized.

But to get back to your question: I'm pretty sure it's not meditation that has got me any closer to living the fact that there's no deep moral responsibility. Insofar as I have got closer, it is just living a life, and the long and devoted practice of philosophy. I think philosophy really does change one over time. It makes one's mind large, in some peculiar manner. It seems to me that the professional practice of philosophy is itself a kind of spiritual discipline, in some totally secular sense of "spiritual"; or at least that it can be, and has been for me. It would be very surprising if intense training of the mind didn't change the shape of the mind as much as intense training of the body changes the shape of the body. It does.

Here's an odd confessional passage from a paper I wrote fifteen years ago that I'd forgotten about until someone mentioned it recently.

> My attitudes on such questions are dramatically inconsistent. For (a) I regard any gifts that I have, and any good that I do, as a matter of pure good fortune; so that the idea that I deserve credit for them in some strong sense seems absurd. But (b) I do not regard others' achievements and good actions as pure good fortune, but feel admiration (and, where appropriate, gratitude) of a true-responsibility-presupposing kind. Furthermore, (c) I do not regard bad things that I do as mere bad luck, but have true-responsibility-presupposing attitudes to them (which may admittedly fade with time). Finally, (d), I do (in everyday life) naturally regard bad things other people do

as explicable in ways that make true-responsibility-presupposing blame inappropriate. I suspect that this pattern may not be particularly uncommon.

TS: Interesting you say that; I would think it *is* pretty uncommon. The idea that we don't deserve credit for our achievements and good deeds? It seems to go against some core American ideals, anyway.

GS: Well, perhaps it's uncommon, but I don't think it's that rare. I agree that it may be pretty un-American, but I don't think it can be that unusual worldwide—or am I the weird one here? One can certainly get a lot of pleasure or happiness from having done something, but taking credit for something does seem absurd, like taking credit or responsibility for one's height or one's looks (putting cosmetic surgery aside). People sometimes say that one can take credit for effort even if one can't take credit for natural talent, but in the end being the kind of person who's got determination and who perseveres and makes an effort—that too is a gift, a piece of luck. It just so happens that we particularly admire it, in the same way that we find some people or landscapes particularly attractive.

TS: And how about (*d*)—the idea that blame is inappropriate for the bad actions of other people?

GS: As for that, I realize that when I wrote it I was thinking of everyday life, not of monstrous acts. (*d*) involves taking what my father called the "objective attitude" to others, and that's certainly how it is for me when it comes to others' wrongdoing in everyday life—at least after the heat of the moment.

III. "IT'S VERY HARD TO IMAGINE THE WORD 'SCHMUCK' ISSUING FROM MY FATHER'S MOUTH."

TS: Let's talk about the objective attitude for a moment. In 1962 your father, P. F. Strawson, wrote a famous paper that continues to haunt anyone working on free will today. In the paper he claims that when you adopt the objective attitude toward another human being, you lose some essential features of interpersonal relationships. You'll start to see this person as an object of social policy, a subject for "treatment"—some Orwellian scenarios come to mind—but you can no longer see them fully as a person. But if we're going to accept the belief that there is no free will, no DMR, it seems we'll have to take the objective attitude toward *all* people, including those closest to us. Are the implications of this as cold and bleak as your father suggests?

GS: No, I don't think so. I disagree that regularly taking the objective attitude toward someone means giving up on treating them fully as a person. In fact I think it's essential to the closest human relations. I think that it is rather a beautiful capability that we have. It is deeply involved in compassion and love. I don't think love is blind. I think love sees all the faults and doesn't mind. It brings the point of view of the universe into our lives, where it is (as far as I can see) welcome. The point of view of the universe can be part of care, caring.

TS: In your book you give one of the most effective critiques I've seen of your dad's paper. What's it like to have a public philosophical disagreement with your father? Has he come around to your point of view or does he just call you a *schmuck* like my dad calls me?

GS: It's very hard to imagine the word *schmuck* issuing from my father's mouth. Perhaps if you got him drunk, passed him a pot of Smucker's jam, and asked him what it was. Actually I've no idea what he thinks about this. I think he might concede the point about the objective attitude and remain content with the deep thought behind his paper, the thought that belief in free will is so deeply built into our natural moral-emotional attitudes to others that philosophical argument about it is simply moot—super-moot. Derek Parfit [a British philosopher famous for his work on personal identity] once said he thought my view was closer to the truth than my father's, but that my father's paper would be the one that would live on. I think he was right. I don't think there's anything oedipal going on. In general, disagreements are fine—real substantive disagreements—because either your opponents are wrong, in which case it's no problem, or they're right, in which case it's also no problem because what's right is right, and what can you do? Plus it's nice to get things right. What's at issue, always, is the truth.

TS: Well, this leads to my next question. In your book you ask us to consider a man who wants to live according to the truth. He wants to consistently deny the existence of free will and DMR. We can imagine that this person will tone down his resentment of others, and maybe he won't be as consumed in self-indulgent bouts of guilt. *But,* you argue, in ordinary situations of choice this man may hit a wall. In these situations, we're *unable* to think that we will be truly or absolutely responsible for our choice, whatever we choose. Granted, there will be an initial impulse on this man's part to see himself as deserving of blame (or praise) for a particular action. On the other hand, he knows that this conception of free will is incoherent and impossible. So the question is: Is it possible that our natures are flexible enough that—after due reflection—this commitment to free will and DMR can be softened, or even eliminated?

GS: I think this question may be the only really interesting question left in the free-will debate, because the answers to the rest are really pretty clear by now. But before I try to answer it let me tell a story that explains why I think we can't help experiencing ourselves as radically free, as having DMR.

Suppose you arrive at a shop on the evening of a national holiday, intending to buy a cake with your last ten-dollar note to supplement the preparations you've already made. Everything is closing down. There's one cake left in the shop; it costs ten dollars. On the steps of the shop someone is shaking an Oxfam tin—or someone is begging, someone who is clearly in distress. You stop, and it seems quite clear to you—it surely *is* quite clear to you—that it is *entirely up to you* what you do next—in such a way that you will have DMR for what you do, whatever you do. The situation is in fact utterly clear: you can put the money in the tin (or give it to the beggar), or you can go in and buy the cake. You're not only completely, radically free to choose in this situation. You're not free not to choose. That's how it feels. You're condemned to freedom, in Sartre's phrase. You're already in a state of full consciousness of what the options are and you can't escape that consciousness. You can't somehow slip out of it.

TS: No matter what your other commitments might be…

GS: Right. You may be convinced that determinism is true: you may believe that in five—two—minutes' time you will be able to look back on the situation you are now in and say truly, of what you will by then have done, "It was determined that I should do that." But even if you do fervently believe this, I still don't think it's going to touch the feeling of DMR that you have right now as you stand there. And although the Oxfam box example is a particularly dramatic one, choices of this general sort are not rare. They occur regularly in our everyday lives.

Well, that's the story; now for the question you asked, the one I thought might be the only really interesting one left. Given that the experience of DMR is seemingly inevitable in our everyday lives, can we shake free of it, can we at least diminish it, can we somehow truly live, breathe the impossibility of DMR, and not just accept it in a merely theoretical context? And is the inevitability of the experience of DMR just a local human fact, a human peculiarity or limitation, or is it going to be inevitable for any possible cognitively sophisticated, rational, self-conscious agent that faces Oxfam-box–type choices and is fully aware of the fact that it does so?

Well, I'm not sure. But I think that perhaps it's not inevitable for human beings, and here I have a couple more quotations I like. The Indian mystical thinker Krishnamurti reports that the experience of radical choice simply fades away when you advance spiritually: "You do not choose," he says, "you do not decide, when you see things very clearly... Only the unintelligent mind exercises choice in life." A spiritually advanced or "truly intelligent mind simply cannot have choice," because it "can... only choose the path of truth." Only the unintelligent mind has free will—by which he means experience of radical free will.

Saul Bellow has a related thought in his novel *Humboldt's Gift:* "In the next realm, where things are clearer, clarity eats into freedom. We are free on earth"—i.e., we experience ourselves as radically free—"because of cloudiness, because of error, because of marvelous limitation." And the great Dutch philosopher Spinoza extends the point to God. God cannot, he says, "be said... to act from freedom of the will." In which case he cannot think or feel that he does so, because he is after all omniscient.

Theology aside, Krishnamurti convinces me that it's not actually impossible for human beings to live the fact that there is no DMR, in spite of the cake and the Oxfam box. What he says has the ring of truth. And there's convergence here with the passage I quoted from Eleanor Rosch's talk. That said, I don't think living without the feeling of DMR is a realistic option for most of us.

IV. BUT CAN I STILL HATE THE YANKEES?

TS: Well, maybe there's *one* more interesting question left in the debate. If living the fact can be done, with hard work, *should* it be done? In other words, if someone accepts the conclusion of the basic argument, that DMR is impossible, would you recommend that he try to live according to this belief?

GS: It might take years of spiritual discipline to get to "living the fact" (though actually one can get quite a ways by ordinary secular reflection). But let's suppose you could achieve it immediately, just by pressing a button. You're asking, Should you press that button?

Well, it might be blissful... but I think it might take you out of the range of normal human relations. You wouldn't mind that consequence once you were there. I'm sure you'd be absolutely clear that it was right to be where you were once you were there. But it might be frightening to contemplate trying to get there, leaving behind all this thick human comforting mess. It might seem bleak from this side, sad, ruling out truly personal relations. I'm not sure it can accommodate romantic love as we ordinarily conceive it. But it would not touch a capacity for compassion, and it would not eliminate reactive attitudes like gratitude, it would just change them deeply from within. It would turn them from moral to aesthetic attitudes. Which, in the end, is all they can properly be.

TS: Really—romantic love is out? I would have thought that love of all kinds remained more or less intact. Why is it necessary to believe in DMR in order to experience romantic love?

GS: Well, with a philosopher's caution, I said romantic love as we ordinarily conceive it. That's because I think the romantic love as we ordinarily conceive it requires the possibility of feeling gratitude, real, freedom-presupposing gratitude, gratitude that has not been deeply changed into a merely aesthetic feeling. That's what I argued in the last chapter of my book *Freedom and Belief*, anyway. But I don't actually think that romantic love, love for a specific individual rather than Christian love, general beneficence, requires the possibility of feeling gratitude. I think it's the same as it was for Michel de Montaigne and his famous profound friendship with Étienne de la Boétie, who died young. When he was asked why their friendship was as it was, he simply said, "Because it was him, because it was me." Same with love. This seems to me deep and true.

Okay, I've answered your question, or I've tried to answer it. Now you must answer my question. Will you or won't you press that button?

TS: I think I'd definitely press it, *if* I had the option of coming back. The one thing I worry about (more than loss of romantic love) is loss of the ability to enjoy sports. That's the one area of my life where

I set all theory aside. When the Red Sox lose, someone's to blame![2]

GS: The way I imagine it, you don't have the option of coming back—but okay, just this once, just for you. But I won't be expecting you back. And you and the Red Sox will be just fine. ✶

---

[2] This interview was published six months before Grady Little single-handedly blew game seven against the Yankees in the 2003 ALCS. In the months that followed, nothing could have convinced me that Little didn't deserve blame for leaving Pedro in the game in the eighth inning.

2

PHILIP ZIMBARDO

"THE POWER OF THE SITUATION."

Put yourself in the following situation. You've agreed to participate in a Yale University study that explores the use of punishment to aid learning and memorization skills. You're randomly assigned the role of "teacher"; the "learner" is strapped to an apparatus in the next room and given a series of memory exercises. Your task as the teacher is to press a lever that sends an electric shock to the learner every time he answers a question incorrectly. The shocks increase in intensity for every incorrect answer—up the scale from Level 1 (15 volts) to Level 13 (195 volts, marked "Very Strong Shock") to Level 25 (375 volts, "Danger—Severe Shock") ending at Level 30 (450 volts, marked "XXX"). The learner you've been paired with is not doing well. He's making a lot of mistakes and has begun complaining about the pain from the shocks. You check with the experimenter and he assures you that it's okay to continue. Still more mistakes. Now the learner screams in pain at every wrong answer. He begs you and the experimenter to let him out. He complains about a heart condition. You're up to level 13 now: 195 volts, "Very Strong Shock." You don't want to continue but the experimenter reminds you that you agreed to do this and claims that he will take full responsibility for whatever happens. The learner screams that you have no right to keep him here. The experimenter asks you firmly to keep going.

What would you do in this situation? Would you take a stand and walk out? Or would you keep pulling the levers, all the way up the scale, past the point where the screaming from the other room has turned into silence....

Many readers will recognize this description as a portrait of the famous Milgram experiments, conducted at Yale in the 1960s by Stanley Milgram.[1] (For those unfamiliar with the study, the "learner" was really an actor, a confederate of the experimenter. The experiment was in fact a study of obedience to authority figures. The shocks were not genuine.) The Milgram experiments presented a deep challenge to American ideas about the power of individual character and free choice. In a follow-up study, Milgram asked subjects to predict how far up the shock scale they would go in this kind of situation. On average, subjects replied that they would refuse to continue after level 10. Nobody said that they would go as far as level 20. When asked to predict the behavior of others, subjects imagined that only 1–2 percent would go all the way to level 30. A group of forty psychiatrists, after hearing about the experiment, agreed with this assessment. After all, only a sadist could repeatedly electrocute an innocent stranger just because a psychologist told them to, right?

Wrong. Both the psychiatrists and the subjects were way off. As it turned out, two out of every three subjects went all the way up to level 30, sending what they believed was 450 volts into the learner in the next room. And once they passed 330 volts, when the learner had stopped screaming and fallen silent (unconscious, or dead perhaps), almost no one stopped until the end. Either two thirds of Connecticut's population are sadists, or bucking authority is much more difficult than we imagine.

---

[1] See Chapter 12 of Philip Zimbardo's *The Lucifer Effect* for a more detailed and dramatic account of the Milgram experiments.

The Milgram study is one of the twin towers of experiments in the "situationist" tradition of studies that reveal the extent to which our circumstances and environment influence human behavior. The other is an equally controversial study known as the Stanford Prison Experiment, conducted by Philip Zimbardo in 1971. A former classmate of Stanley Milgram's at James Monroe High School in the Bronx, Dr. Zimbardo wanted to study the effects of a prison environment on human behavior. He gathered a group of college students, randomly divided them into "prisoners" and "guards," and placed them in a simulated prison at Stanford University. What followed is discussed at some length in the interview below; for now, it's enough to say that the behavior was so unexpectedly brutal and dehumanizing that the experiment—designed to last two weeks—had to be cut short after only six days. So when Zimbardo heard about the abuses at Abu Ghraib, and then saw the notorious photographs, he says he wasn't surprised. He had seen this pattern of abuse before—the sexual humiliation, naked prisoners with bags over their heads—in his own simulated prison! And when the Bush administration depicted the abuses as the actions of "a few bad apples," Zimbardo could say with some authority that a "bad barrel"—twelve-hour shifts without a day off, fatigue, stress, ambiguous orders from above, a systematic lack of leadership, and the prison itself—was likely the more important contributing factor. After hearing him interviewed on NPR about the scandal, the attorney for Chip Frederick, one of the guards at Abu Ghraib, asked Zimbardo to serve as an expert witness for the defense. This experience prompted Zimbardo to write a book, *The Lucifer Effect,* about the Abu Ghraib abuses, the power of situational elements to influence behavior, and, for the first time ever, a detailed, reflective, and fascinating account of the Stanford Prison Experiment conducted almost forty years earlier.

Philip Zimbardo is professor emeritus of psychology at Stanford University. I met him at his house just off the zigzagged portion of Lombard Street in San Francisco. Over scones and tea, looking out at the bay, we discussed the prison experiment and its implications for ethics, responsibility, free will, and social policy.

February 2009

I. "WE GOT OFF ON BEING PUPPETEERS."

TAMLER SOMMERS: What was the original purpose for doing the Stanford Prison Experiment? What did you want to demonstrate or discover?

PHILIP ZIMBARDO: It was 1971 and a time of enormous social change in our country, especially in California, where a lot of social movements started. The hippies, the love-ins, the be-ins, the beat poets—all of it was here. There was a strong antiwar movement; I was heavily involved in that. I was involved when I was at NYU, and then again when I got to Stanford. And one of the big issues was questioning authority, rebelling against it. Don't trust authority, don't trust anyone over thirty—you know, the big signs: FUCK AUTHORITY, OINK OINK: AGAINST THE PIGS. And the question is: how much of that is rhetoric? Do we have a new generation of independent free thinkers?

A little less than a decade earlier, at Yale, Stanley Milgram demonstrated the enormous power that situations can have on seducing ordinary people into a role where, although they thought they were teachers, they really ended up almost *executioners* of a stranger. Milgram's study, though it was really important, was about authority's pressure on an individual. My reasoning is that this rarely happens in the world. Authorities dictate, give general orders, or an ideology, and it filters down through systems in various ways, and then low-level people carry it out. But most of our lives are in institutions, in families, in schools, in hospitals, in armies, in teams… and institutions have a different kind of power. It's an institutional power, systemic power.

TS: Higher-level influences?

PZ: Yeah, it's not people telling you to do this bad thing. It's creating a general ideology, a general orientation, a way of thinking about things. And there're sets of rules and laws and a focus that moves people in a certain direction, and you have group conformity, and you have group-think. That's the reason I did the Stanford prison study. In a sense, it was like Milgram's study, in that it was an attempt to demonstrate how powerful social situations can be when pitted against the individual will to resist, the individual's sense of willpower and freedom. In that sense, they're really bookends of what's come to be known as "the power of the situation." His is one-on-one; mine is institutional power.

TS: And this experiment could broaden our understanding of the power of situational elements.

PZ: It's really to broaden his message and put it to a higher-level test. In Milgram's study, we don't know about those thousand people who answered the ad. His subjects weren't Yale students, though he did it at Yale. They were a thousand ordinary citizens from New Haven and Bridgeport, Connecticut, ages twenty to fifty. In his advertisement in the newspaper he said: college students and high-school students cannot be used. It could have been a selection of people who were more psychopathic. For our study, we only picked two dozen of seventy-five who applied, those who scored normal or average on seven different personality tests. So we knew there were no psychopaths, no deviants. Nobody had been in therapy, and even though it was a drug era, nobody (at least in the reports) had taken anything beyond marijuana, and they were physically healthy at the time. So the question was: suppose you only had kids who were normally healthy, psychologically and physically, and they knew they would be going into a prisonlike environment and that some of their civil rights would be sacrificed. Would those good people put in that bad, evil place—would their goodness triumph? It should have!

TS: You mean, given our conception of human behavior?

PZ: Right. They should have had some inner sense of character and integrity, not to get seduced into mindless obedience and mindless conformity. To be able to say, "Hey, that's the role, it's not me. I'm this other person, I'm this college student, I'm this anti-war activist, I'm this civil-rights activist."

TS: But as it turned out…

PZ: Even when we preselect for intelligent, normal, healthy, young men, that doesn't minimize the power of the situation.

TS: I read that the focus of the study was going to be mostly about the prisoners, more than the guards. Since then, interest in the study has in large part shifted to the guards.

PZ: When we got the idea to do the study, yes. More about the prisoners. To prepare for the research, I taught a course in the psychology of imprisonment with an ex-convict, a guy named Carlo Prescott, who later became the consultant for this study. He had just been released from prison after seventeen years. In our course we brought in ex-convicts and guards and prison chaplains. And so my sympathies were heavily with prisoners. I was antiprisons, anticorrections, etc. We really wanted to understand the socialization of becoming a prisoner; what's happening. Essentially, we were, at some personal, Hollywood level, pulling for the prisoners to be able to resist.

TS: Hoping that they'd all be Cool Hand Luke, to one degree or another.

PZ: They'd be Cool Hand Luke, or they'd pretend to go along with it. When we bugged the cells we could say, "Oh, we're faking this thing." After the first day, we were ready to call it quits, because nothing was happening. Everybody felt awkward. But then what became apparent was the ingenuity of the guards. It was the guards that were going to make this thing work or not work. The key was the morning of the second day, when the prisoners rebelled. They were saying "Fuck you," they were cursing at the guards, they were ripping off their numbers, you know, "We're people!" It was like all those protest marches. "I'm a man," that kind of thing. I was really happy. The guards came to me and said, "What are we gonna do?" I said, "It's your prison; make the decision." They said, "Well, we need support." So they called in the other shifts. But now the guards on the morning shift started dumping on the other shift— "How did you let this happen?" So suddenly egos are involved, and the whole shift is embarrassed. So now that they have twelve guards, they break down the doors, they strip the prisoners naked. There was some physical struggle, and they got the ringleaders of the rebellion and put them in solitary.

TS: And that was when all the degradation started?

PZ: Normally, there were only three guards and nine prisoners. But each shift realized that [the rebellion] could happen again on their shift. The first thing they said was, "I realize now these are dangerous prisoners." So they were going to have to use tactics. They organized a good cell and a bad cell. The prisoners in the good cell were going to get privileges. Then they said, "Everything is a privilege," short of breathing air. Food is a privilege.

TS: Was there a sort of taste of having this power over someone else, this authority?

PZ: I think that came secondarily. I think it was the fear first, that this could happen at any time. It took us by surprise, and it was embarrassing for that shift. Then all the other guards thought, It could happen on my shift, then I would be responsible. But saying that they were dangerous prisoners meant that they were no longer experimental subjects. I think the sense of power came after they began to ratchet up the control. To say, "Okay, now, we're going to have these counts go on for hours on end. We're going to arbitrarily show that we're in control. I tell a joke, you laugh, I punish you. I tell a joke, you don't laugh, I punish you." I think the sense of power came after the display of domination and control, in that guards began to feel that, Yeah, I can do this, I can get away with it. And then once the prisoners gave in even slightly, then they just kept amping it up.

TS: This is jumping ahead, but didn't you quote Charles Graner [the Abu Ghraib ringleader] as saying something like: "Part of me thought this was terrible, that what I'm doing is humiliating another person, but part of me just likes to see a prisoner piss his pants"?

PZ: In fact, Graner said that the Christian in him knew it was wrong, while the other part... wanted to see a guy pissing his pants. There's a movie called the *Human Behavior Experiments*, by Alex Gibney. He's the one who won the Oscar for *Taxi to the Dark Side*. And he looked at the Milgram study and the Stanford prison study, and he interviewed some of the participants from the Stanford study. He interviewed the guard they called John Wayne, who's now a mortgage broker in the suburbs someplace. So Gibney asks John Wayne about Abu Ghraib. John Wayne says, Given the time, we could have gotten there. You know, we were almost there. And then he says something like, "We got off on having them be our puppets," or "We got off on being puppeteers." It really was that sense of total control. It's like *Pinocchio*. It's frightening, but it's also insightful to say, "Look how far we came in five days."

II. TAKING ON THE ROLES
WE'RE ASSIGNED

TS: Another really interesting part of your book is your fairly detailed description of the situation's impact on *you*. Philip Zimbardo as the prison superintendent. My favorite example in the book is after one of the prisoners broke down and you had to release him, and you thought he was going to lead a prison break-in. So you started to get obsessed with this prison break-in and you're trying to reach the chief of police. The officer thinks you're a nutcase.

PZ: Right, the "psycho psychologist."

TS: A visiting colleague later asked you a normal question for a psychologist: What's the independent variable here? Let me read this; this is great. You get angry. "Here I had an incipient riot on my hands. The security of my men and the stability of my prison were at stake, and I had to contend with this bleeding heart, liberal, academic, effete professor whose only concern was a ridiculous thing like an independent variable. You effete liberal academic, I have a break-in on my hands, what are you talking about, 'independent variable'?"

PZ: And that was only the third day! Of course, it was all a rumor, there was no break-in. But see, I had been doing research on rumor transmission. And now there was a rumor of a break-in. I was the psychologist! I should have said, "Great, we're gonna study this." And if there *was* a break-in, that would have been a very dramatic thing: what would happen, and how would you deal with it? But at that point I had become the prison superintendent, and the only interest you have is your institution. The administrator cares about the institution, the integrity of the institution, and its staff. That's where, you know, I really switched over to being focused more on the institution, the agenda, the itinerary, and the guards.

TS: So you brought the prisoners up to the classroom...

PZ: The fifth-floor storage room, actually. It was terrible. It was this dark room. There were bags over their heads for hours and hours. I was sitting there, too, so it was wasting time. Nothing happened. We didn't collect data on the rumor transmission, we just wasted all this time. But did we all realize how stupid we were? No, we blame it on the prisoners. We thought that somebody must have spread that rumor to get us upset. So then the guards said, "Okay, we're going to ratchet up the abuse of the prisoners. We're going to keep them up longer, counts are going to be two hours at a time, push-ups will be doubled, and so forth. Put them in solitary confinement for longer periods for any infraction." That was transformative for me, but I still didn't realize it. It's not like I stepped back and said, "Oh, my god, look at you."

TS: At any point did you have a kind of awareness that you were getting sucked into it, or did that only come afterward?

PZ: No. Well—it came out partially when prisoner 819... he was beginning to have an emotional breakdown. When the chaplain was interviewing him among the others, he started crying, you know, hysterically, and at that point I thought the chaplain was going to say, "Blow the whistle, look, this is out of control." In fact, he told me later, he said, "Oh, that's a first-offender reaction, that is, they're all very emotional initially and they have to learn not to do that because they're going to look like sissies, they're going to get abused." But then 819 went ballistic, he started ripping up his pillow, his mattress and shit, and they put him in solitary confinement. And his cellmates got punished for not limiting that. He's now hysterical and one of the guards comes and says, "We think he's breaking down." So I brought him up to a recreation room for the cameramen and observers. When prisoners were going to be released we brought them there to settle down before we took them to student health. So I bring this guy there, 819, and I'm saying, "Okay, 819, look, time is up, we're going pay you for the whole time," and so forth, and just then the guards line up the prisoners and get them to chant: "819 is a bad prisoner. Because of what 819 did my cell is a mess. I'm being punished for 819."

Now this guy starts crying again and says, "I've got to go back! I've got to go back and prove I'm not a bad prisoner." And so that was a shock. And so I said, "Wait a minute, you're not a prisoner, you're not 819, this is an experiment, you're a student, your name is Stewart." And at that point I said, "And I'm Phil Zimbardo." He said, "Okay, okay." And I escorted the student out. But saying: "I'm not the superintendent. I'm this other person..."

TS: It was almost as much of a discovery for you as it was for him?

PZ: Yeah, so it was... But then you get sucked back in.

TS: Even the peripheral people, right? The parents, the chaplain...

PZ: Yes. The chaplain was there because he came to see me, he wanted some references for a paper he was doing on violence or something, and then he told me he had been a prison chaplain. And I said, "Hey, I'm going to do this experiment, could you come down and give me a validity check?" So he was in my office and he came down and he's treating me like I'm the superintendent. And so he was really at fault—he definitely should have blown the whistle at that point.

TS: At fault in one sense, right? Like everyone else, wasn't he also just sucked into his role?

PZ: Yeah, he was sucked into the role. The kid was breaking down; this was after three days. And the chaplain says, "Oh, it's very realistic, what you're doing. Good simulation." The amazing thing with him was that during meetings with the prisoners, he asked them: "What're you doing when you get out?" And they said, "What do you mean, sir?" "Well, you're in a prison." So he actually reinforced it, because he was an outsider. And he told them they would need a lawyer if they wanted to get out. And one kid said, "Well, you know, I'm gonna go to law school. I can defend myself." And the chaplain says, "Lawyers who defend themselves have a fool for a client." And then he says, "Would you like me to get you help?" And the kid says, "Yeah." The kid gives him his mother's name, and he calls. So there was this bizarre thing. He calls the mother and says, "Your son needs a lawyer." Now that he's trapped in his priest role, he made a promise to the kid. Rather than calling to say, "Hey, your son is in this experiment, he's having a hard time dealing with it, maybe you should take him out." In one sense, the ethics of the priest should have been, you know, he told the kid he would help, but he was so narrowly focused on what he said—"I will get you a lawyer"—that he told the mother to get him a lawyer. The mother calls a cousin, and this public defender actually comes in.

TS: The parents went along with all of this as well, right?

PZ: Yes. One of the rules was that on visiting days, visiting nights, parents had to see the warden first, and then the superintendent on their way out. The reason we did this is because we wanted to bring their behavior in the situation under control. So essentially, these were good middle-class parents, and they were following the rules. They signed in, they sat down, they saw the warden, they went in, they saw the superintendent. And they just fell into it.

The other story, which was very moving, was this couple who came out after seeing their son. He was in really bad shape. The mother began right off: "I don't mean to make trouble, sir"— that's the other thing, the "sir." You see, usually they'd say "doctor" or "professor," but "sir"—"but I've never seen my son looking so bad." As soon as I heard, "I don't mean to make trouble," a red light went on in my head: She's going to make trouble. So she's trouble—not to the experiment, to the prison. And so I said, "What seems to be your son's problem?"

TS: Your *son's* problem..

PZ: Yes, right, so here the whole experiment was about the power of the situation over the dispositional personal attributions. She's saying, "There's something bad about this situation." As an administrator, I'm saying: "What's wrong with your kid?" She says, "Well, he doesn't sleep." I said, "Does he have insomnia?" So I'm putting the problem onto *him,* not the situation. And she says, "No, no, they wake them up every few hours." And I said, "Oh, that, that's called the counts." I run through this whole thing, and I tell her why it's essential, and the husband's just sitting there, real quiet and really upset because his wife is challenging authority. She says again, "I don't mean to make trouble." And so I think she's going to blow the whistle. I automatically did something that is so horrific, and against all my values: I just turn to the father and say, "Don't you think your boy can handle a little stress?"

TS: Ah, so that he'll…

PZ: What's he going to say—"My boy's a sissy"? He's gotta say, "Of course. He's a tough guy, he's a leader." I stood up immediately. He stood up. We shook hands. I said, "I'll see you next visiting hour. Good work, sir."

TS: So you played on the father's fear that it would be his son's weakness, rather than the situation, if he had to quit.

PZ: Essentially what I did was say, "Here's this woman who's soft. And we men have to stick together." And yes: What does it say about your son, and therefore what does it say about his father? I mean, you want to say that your son is a sissy? He can't handle it? But it was automatic, it wasn't a strategic thing. I mean, this was instantaneous. We have all that knowledge stored. So we did the handshake thing. The son broke down that night and the next day I got a letter—I think I have it in the book—I got a letter the next day from the mother saying, "Thank you very much, it's really very interesting, I'm still concerned about my son." Meanwhile, he had broken down. So she was right on.

TS: Another fascinating description from the book is Carlo. Carlo was himself a prisoner on parole, right? He was a consultant for the study, and then you had him leading the parole board. You'd think that if anyone would be sensitive to the sort of suffering that goes with being in front of a parole board, it would be Carlo. And yet he jumped into the role with both feet.

PZ: It's interesting. Nobody's really mentioned Carlo. Nobody cared for that. And it's a really powerful thing. Here's a guy who'd had his parole denied for seventeen years. That means every year you come up, once a year, you have three to five minutes to plead your case, you do your thing, and you get turned down. And you don't know why. They don't tell you why. Just—you got turned down. So he'd recently been paroled, and his sympathy should have been with the prisoners, no question about it. But now he's the head of the parole board. And it was brilliant. I think we have a little bit of it on video. He had a blank pad, and he picks it up and says "I see here from your rap sheet that you're a troublemaker." He was reading from it, he was very creative and very eloquent. All the dialogue from the book is actually from the audio tape. Again, here was a guy who hated prisons, who went into a rage about what prisons did to him. In prison, he saw people break down. And we put him in that role, and he says, "You're a troublemaker. It says here that you said this and this about this guard and that. You're a threat to the community. I don't see how we can release you. What do you expect to do when you get out?" The kid says, "I want to be a teacher." He says, "I wouldn't want you teaching my children." Carlo didn't have kids. And so, in one way it was this brilliant improvisation but it was horrendous because he was as evil as a parole officer. And for each one, he said, "Forget it. There's no way. Get out. If it was up to me, I'd leave you here forever." One kid came back in; he went out and came back in and begged him, said, "You know, I'm sorry, I was too flippant," and so forth.

TS: What did Carlo say to that? Something really cutting, I remember that.

PZ: It was an Asian kid. Carlo said something like, "We don't usually get people of your race here." And that day this kid got a full psychosomatic rash, you know, over his whole body. We had to release him.

TS: This is also amazing—the parole board lasted two days, and Carlo felt terrible about it the first night. So then, you'd think, Okay, finally, he realizes... But then he was back full force the next day.

PZ: Again, you're physically out of the situation. You're saying, "Oh my god, was that me?" But the next day I think was the more hardcore part. He just went right back into it. He told me afterward, when the whole thing was over, "When I think back it makes me sick." But it's exactly like [Abu Ghraib guard] Chip Fredrick. I don't know why he did it. You can't verbalize it, you can't say, "Oh, I was being given that status of power, I was showing off to the other people there." Really what Carlo had encrypted was all of the power, the authority. The same way he hated it when he got turned down. And now you give him the power and what does he do?

III. LEARNED HELPLESSNESS

TS: So, let's turn to the prisoners for a moment. We talked about how the guards got off on having control of the prisoners. From the interviews of the prisoners afterward, it seems like the worst part of the experience for them was the *loss* of control, being at the arbitrary whim of these guards—the arbitrariness of what would happen to them. They'd be in the good prison cell if they did bad things, the bad prison cell if they did good things. Can you elaborate on why that's such a horrible thing?

PZ: You know, I just realized this for the first time. The last book I did was called *The Time Paradox*. And it's really about how people divide the flow of their experience into time zones: past, present, and future. And I just thought, for the very first time, I don't know why, that is what happened to the prisoners. They got into this "present fatalism" mode.

TS: Present fatalism?

PZ: Nothing I do makes a difference. My life is controlled, fated. My life is controlled by the guards. And it's totally arbitrary. So there's a sense of learned helplessness. That's the underlying concept. The original study was by Marty Seligman of the University of Pennsylvania. You put dogs in a situation where they get shocked until they press up a bar on the door, the door opens, then they escape. But then you change the situation. Now when they press the bar, nothing happens. And sometimes when they stop pressing, the door opens. So now nothing they do makes any difference. They can escape without pressing the bar, they press the bar, nothing. And what happens is: they give up. They just stop.

They lay down and they take the shock. It's a learned helplessness. It's not built into the system, not genetic. We're genetically designed to survive. But once you learn that your behavior does not control important consequences, you stop behaving. And that's essentially what happened there. The guards—and they never all got together, they all did it in various ways, different shifts. They created an arbitrary environment where there was no predictability; you couldn't predict what was the right or the wrong answer. It's that sense of fatalism: I don't control outcomes. And one of the most central aspects of human nature is the perception that I have reasonable control over my life, that if I do *a*, then *b* is gonna follow in a reasonable amount of time. And the more I do *a,* and *b* doesn't happen, then I try *c.* So I keep changing my behavior to get the desired outcomes. If nothing I do ever gets a desired outcome, I stop doing anything and I stop desiring the outcome. I stop desiring freedom, or whatever. It's a horrendous condition.

TS: One of the striking things—I guess this is analogous to the dogs finally not even taking steps to get out—was the prisoners accepting the judgment during the "parole hearings." You even asked them: "Look, if, *if* I offered you the opportunity to leave, but you had to forfeit your money, would you do that?" A lot of them said yes! They forgot that they could do this *at any time* and probably still get the money, any time they wanted. And yet, when the judgment didn't go their way…

PZ: They stood up, they put their hands out, put their handcuffs on. And here now, again, the parole board, we purposely did it… it was on a different floor, it was in a big laboratory classroom, there were people not connected with the experiment on the parole board, so it wasn't like the prisoners were locked in that chamber, but they carried the situation around in their heads. And so, once we said "We'll consider your parole," when Carlo said, "Take 'em away," it was just this automatic thing. They put the bags over their heads. When they *should* have said, "Hey, the only reason I'm in this study, and the only reason people said to be in it, was for the money." It wasn't that they were interested in prison life; they weren't psychology students. And the guards took them away. Also, at that point, the guards were at their worst.

TS: You focus a lot of criticism in the book on your role in the experiment. Here's a sort of emblematic quote: "Only a few people were able to resist the situational temptations to yield to power and dominance while maintaining some semblance of morality and decency; obviously I was not among that noble class." Why are you so hard on yourself?

PZ: Well, yeah, because I deserve it! I was the adult, they were kids. I had done lots of research. I should not have allowed myself to get so trapped in that role. The whole study is about the power of the situation; I mean, that abstract concept should have been there to say, "Hey, look, here's that thing you're studying, and here you are caught up in it." And I kept coming close to it, with 819, with the prison break, but I kept being drawn back in. When one of the prisoners broke down, I should have said, "Look, that's enough." The mother was right. And I humiliated her.

One day Christina Maslach came down and saw the guards line up the prisoners for the toilet run at ten o'clock. The guards chained the prisoners' legs together, the prisoners have their bags over their head, their arms on each other. The guards are cursing and yelling at them, the prisoners are shuffling along. I look up and I have the day's agenda—and I check off *ten o'clock toilet run*. That's all it is. She looks at it and says, "This is horrendous! This is dehumanization. This is a violation of everything that humanity stands for. And you're allowing this to happen, essentially." So that was a really critical thing. I wasn't being cruel, I was just being totally indifferent to suffering. And indifferent to suffering because what was happening is what usually happened at ten o'clock. If it didn't happen, *then* I would have been concerned: "Where's the ten o'clock toilet run?" The toilet run didn't have to be with chains, it didn't have to be with bags, it didn't have to be with all this other stuff. But that got to be the routine. So we're following a routine, it's nothing more than a checking off, for me. For her, it was nothing less than a violation of humanity.[2]

IV. PUTTING THE SITUATION ON TRIAL.

TS: This experiment and a lot of others in social psychology expose something that's called the "fundamental attribution error." Can you explain what that is, exactly?

PZ: In all individualistic societies, our analyses tend to be focused on individual personality. Character is what's important, free will is what's important. Characters in novels, characters in movies. We have heroes and villains. We identify the person as the instigator of the action, whether good or bad. And this is true through all of our institutions, so individuals get credit for success, individuals get blame for failure. Law deals only with individuals. Medicine, aside from public health, deals only with individuals. Religion, sins of individuals. So all of our institutions deal with individuals. Even economics is the "rational man theory," which proves to be totally irrational.[3]

So because of that, we're conditioned from early childhood, in those societies, that when we're trying to understand the cause of any given behavior, we attribute the cause to something inside the person. Motives, values, beliefs, genetics. And when we want to change undesirable behavior, we focus on changing the individual. And so if the behavior is undesirable, we reeducate, we imprison, we medicate, we segregate, we sterilize, we execute individuals. And at the same time—the fundamental attribution error has two parts—we underestimate the power of the social context, the social situation. So we overestimate how important the person is, we underestimate how important the situation is. That's the fundamen-

---

[2] Zimbardo and Christina Maslach were married the next year.

[3] See my interview with Joe Henrich (Chapter 5) for more on the "rational man" or *Homo economicus* model of human behavior.

tal attribution error.

TS: You say that this is a problem particularly in an individualistic country like the US. Would you say that more collectivist cultures—in southeast Asia, for example—have a more accurate understanding of human behavior precisely because they take social context more into account?

PZ: Yeah, I think a collectivist orientation simply says, You have to be aware that individuals are always impacted by others, by the family, by social mores, by social rules of being. So when understanding any behavior, collectivists are not primed to say, "Let's look at the individual." There are lots of very simple studies that, you know, show animation of fish swimming, and there's a school of fish, and then there's one fish that's separated, either swimming ahead or behind. When Americans look at that, they focus on the isolated fish, and say he's falling behind. Asians focus on the school of fish, and say they slowed down to let him catch up.

TS: Let's talk about this issue of responsibility. And here I'm almost certain that I'm going to come at this from maybe another side than you normally get. It seemed in other interviews that people were worried about your work being a *threat* to moral responsibility and free will. And often, it seems, you assured them that it isn't. You say a few times in the book, "I'm not saying they're not responsible, this isn't 'excusology'—they're still responsible for their immoral behavior." In one interview I think you even used the phrase "ultimately responsible." My take here is the opposite. It seems like your work *does* undermine moral responsibility.[4] I mean, look at the Stanford Prison Experiment. It was a coin toss that led the guards to be where they were. How can we hold people responsible for bad luck, for a bad coin toss?

---

[4] See my interview with Galen Strawson (Chapter 1) for some thoughts on why this might not be such a terrible implication.

PZ: It's really a very complicated and central issue that needs to be dealt with more. I think philosophers have to deal with it more— it's really a philosophical and legal issue. In the extreme case, it really is a matter of "the situation made me do it." So are we going to put the situation on trial? Well, we don't have a mechanism. I gave a talk at Harvard Law School and [Harvard psychologist] Jon Hanson said that these ideas should provoke a revolution in legal theory because we have no way of putting the situation on trial. In a sense, international tribunals put the system on trial. They have individuals, but that's the real importance of international tribunals for crimes against humanity. They say that even though within your system it was acceptable for you to do this—to kill Jews, or to kill Tutsis— there's a higher international standard of humanity, of justice, that applies, and so it's that ultimate system which dominates your parochial system, your Nazi system, your Communist system, etc.

TS: As you say, though, it's the individuals who are being tried.

PZ: Yes, even there, you know, what comes out of that is the guilt or innocence of each of the leaders. So tribunals say "We have the power to put leaders on trial, even though none of them actually killed anybody—it's just that they created a policy, they created a system." But I would hope they would go the next level and make it explicit: "In punishing this person, we are publicly declaring that this ideology produced the crimes against humanity. And so we, as an international body of humanists, of jurists, decry the horrors of this kind of system." So you're really sending out a message: it's the system that's wrong, and these people helped create it. Hitler helped create it, and Pol Pot… But once it's created, once the Stanford Prison Experiment was created, I'm irrelevant. If I had died during the thing, it would have gone on. The guards would have been happier. If Hitler had been killed, the whole thing would have gone on only because it had already corrupted the legal system, the educational system, the business system. With all these mechanisms in place, he became irrelevant. In fact, he would have been a big martyr.

TS: That's interesting—you know, there's a philosophical view of punishment that's called the "expressivist theory of punishment"— they say that the goal of punishment is not to give people what they deserve, which is hard to make sense of, and not just to deter future crime, but to publicly express your condemnation of an act. Punishment is the only way to express moral condemnation of an act or a system. If you don't punish the culprits, you're sending an implicit message that the act is morally acceptable. And I suppose you could apply that to responsibility, that that's the new way to look at responsibility, as expressing our condemnation.[5]

PZ: Yeah, most punishment does not deter, except for a very short time. There are so many multiple factors that go into producing any kind of crime that a deterrent effect can't have that much influence. In fact, most people don't even know that someone got arrested in New Hampshire, or Arizona, or Alaska for something and is on death row. So how can it be a deterrent for me here in San Francisco? But the notion that we as a society want to express our revulsion about this kind of act makes sense—that it's an expression of a public consensus that this is wrong and that we will not tolerate it. And that's what I'm saying. International tribunals should make explicit that what we're expressing is this revulsion about a system that could create these crimes against humanity. And the way we're doing it is by singling out people who were instrumental in carrying out the policies of that system.

V. "FREE WILL IS AN ILLUSION."

TS: Let's talk about the free-will question for a moment. In the interviews I've heard, you seem to try to dodge questions about free will.

PZ: Yes.

---

[5] Note that if you viewed moral responsibility in this manner, it would not be vulnerable to the argument Galen Strawson presents in Chapter One. People would not have to be responsible for who they are in order to be responsible for their actions.

TS: On the other hand, you say repeatedly that we have this infinite capacity for good and evil, but that who we are is shaped by our situation and circumstances. This relates also to the question of the different levels of situation and system. So where would our free will be in all of this? I know that some people will say that free will is located more in deciding what kind of situations we create for ourselves and others. But aren't those decisions then also determined by other situations, other circumstances?

PZ: There could be an infinite regress. I can see what you're getting at. I mean, free will is something that people really want to believe in. It's the inner individual control over his or her fate. Certainly individualist societies really want to believe in it. We want to believe—that's the most fundamental motivation. I did it because I chose to do it. In fact, one reason the book doesn't sell[6] is that nobody wants to hear this argument. It's just alien to what it means to be a citizen, to be a person. We say we act out of free will. In fact, in Chip Frederick's trial, I'm sure the prosecutor at some point asked: Do you mean they didn't *choose* to perform these acts? The prosecutor couldn't even understand what the situationist argument meant. It violates everything… how could a soldier not have free will? So I think that's the problem. We place such a high value on the belief that individuals act out of free will, act out of personal choice, that their behavior is not determined by anything outside of them…

But I think it's an illusion. I just read a great quote this morning—something like, "I don't believe in God, but I miss him."[7] I don't know who said that, but it's like… I don't really believe in free will, but I can't live without it. I can't live without the belief. I think it's about the dignity of individuals.

TS: But it's an illusion nevertheless.

---

[6] Zimbardo's *The Lucifer Effect* did, however, make it to number 11 on the *New York Times* best-seller list.

[7] The quotation appears in Julian Barnes's *Nothing to Be Frightened Of* (2008).

PZ: I think I would have to say free will is an illusion. A lot of control is an illusion. Advertisers give you an illusion of control: You're choosing Kellogg's Corn Flakes over another brand because... Or take all the cigarette companies. Their whole thing was freedom of choice—that the anti-smoking fanatics are taking away your freedom of choice, and you have the freedom to choose to smoke whenever you want, wherever you want. So it's giving people an illusion of choice. I did a whole set of research in dissonance theory, where we got people to take painful electric shocks, really painful electric shocks. And we said, "Of course, you don't have to do it. If you choose to go on, remember, it's your free choice." I think we used those words. And they said yes. They're strapped into this thing, I'm standing with a lab coat over them, they're in a little cubicle, I'm the professor, they're the student, it's an experiment. Half of them refused, but the other half said, "Yes, I'll go on." The truth is there was no choice. That's the way we manipulated it. But if they agreed, thinking they made a free choice, then they psychologically perceived the shock as less painful.

TS: It doesn't hurt as much as it would have if they hadn't thought they made the choice?

PZ: Right. And physiologically, they react as if it were less painful. And we have control groups where we lower the shock by twenty volts and physiologically they lower the shock by twenty volts. They have no free choice. We arrange it so that they're going to go on. We know they're going to go on. And just saying "Remember, you have a free choice, you don't have to do it, right?"—as soon as they say "Right," then they change. They say, I don't have to do this. And they're taking electric shocks and "Gee, it's not so bad." So the dissonance is: you agree to do something which you know is not good for you. But if you believe you chose to do it, then you perceive, you rationalize why it should be good for you.

TS: Rationalizing at the physiological level—that's fascinating. I read about another experiment like that where they gave two groups a very tedious task. One group got paid a lot, the other hardly anything. The people who got money for it droned on about how boring it was. The people who got almost nothing didn't complain....

PZ: That's Festinger and Carlsmith. That's one of the very first experiments in dissonance theory. So if you got a lot of money for it, then you were extra-aggrieved. You complained. If you only received ten cents, and nothing in later studies, then you said, "Oh no, it was interesting."

TS: You have to justify it to yourself.

PZ: And you believe it. I did a lot of that research. I have a whole book called *The Cognitive Control of Motivation,* which has all these studies. We've done things with hunger. You become less hungry if you agree. You have people who say, "You can't eat anything for twenty-four hours." Then you come in, fill out some questionnaire, then you say, "Okay, now, in some conditions, we're asking some people to go another twenty-four hours. You don't have to do it if you don't want to. I can't even give you any more money to do it." But if they agree to do it they become less hungry. I mean, physiologically measured they become less hungry. The moment they agree to do something they don't really want to do.

TS: It's also interesting because it seems like there's a sort of misperception of the kind of control that we actually want. The prisoners in your experiment were upset about their lack of control over the situation. But what they wanted wasn't this illusory kind of control that probably doesn't exist. They just wanted to make decisions that led to outcomes they could predict. And we normally have that. That's the kind of control we hate to lose, and maybe we misinterpret that as a kind of ultimate control.

PZ: Ultimately, you want control of outcomes. You want to be able to say, "Here's what I'm going to do today. I'm going to do this and this and this and this, I'm going to go and buy something." I don't expect to go down to the store and say "I want to buy something" and the guy says "I don't want you in my store, you look dangerous," or "I'm going to call the police, don't touch the food." Suddenly you're not controlling the outcomes, because here's some things you didn't expect. I guess what I'm saying is that we do want to have real control, and in the absence of that, we're willing to accept illusions of control. We're willing to accept the belief that we are controlling, and then psychologically we do control. We say "I'm less hungry," "It's less shocking," "It's not going to hurt so much," "I feel really good about that." And that's where we become manipulable by advertisers, by salesmen, by wheelers and dealers. Because it's so important for us to have control. And where we don't have real control somebody can just say, "Hey, by voting for me, you're exercising your control." "By smoking Camels, un-filtered, that shows you're a real man, you're in control."

TS: *You're* making the choice.

VI. "YOU CAN'T WIN A WAR ON NOUNS."

TS: This talk of responsibility and control reminds of the quote by Condoleezza Rice you cite in the book. She's explicitly denying the power of situtationist elements to influence people like terror-ists. She puts it all on them, on the wickedness of their characters: "When are we going to stop making excuses for the terrorists and saying that someone is making them do it? No, these are simply evil people that want to kill."

PZ: Right—I was furious! Here's this supposed intellect, and she says "They're just evil people." And you guys [the Bush adminis-tration] aren't evil, you guys are saying, Rice especially, "We don't want the smoking gun to be a mushroom cloud." She's saying if we didn't do this [the war on terror] we could have a nuclear bomb go off in the US.

TS: You're very hard on her in the book. The whole Bush administration really, and Rumsfeld and Cheney especially.

PZ: God, yes!

TS: I want to play devil's advocate and ask whether in their own way, they were trapped in the situation as well. Which led them to institute their policies. It's a little harder to figure out the details of their situation because there's so much we don't know, but isn't it reasonable to assume that they were in one just as much as—

PZ: No, but in their case, they helped create the situation.

TS: That's true, but in doing so, weren't they also part of a larger situation that led them to create the situation in Abu Ghraib?

PZ: The abuses in Abu Ghraib are one thing. But I'm saying they were the principals in creating the whole—I don't know what the broadest context is—the war on terror. That is, Cheney primarily, and Bush and Rumsfeld and George Tenet. For very conscious, aware reasons, they decided to label the global challenge of terrorism— which it should have been called—a *war* on terrorism, so that Bush could be the active commander in chief, so they could have martial law, so they could suspend lots of rights. That's why it's called "the war on terror." And you can't win a war on nouns! We lost a war on drugs, we lost a war on poverty, we're losing a war on terror. It's not clear if verbs win or adjectives win. So I hold them responsible because they set up the system; they are the Hitler and Goebbels and Goering. Each of them said, "Here's my domain, and I'm going to run it this way, and we're not allowing alternative views. Saying that anyone who criticizes us is putting our boys and soldiers in harm's way, anybody who criticizes us is unpatriotic. They set up all these mechanisms, to say, you know, you're feeding the enemy— you're killing the soldiers by protesting against it. And then they essentially instituted—because of this unique power base—the NSA secret thing, they're spying on us, they have these renditions, torture things, a whole set of things that are alien to everything, all basic

American values. The military commissions act, which they pushed through, overturns two hundred years of Anglo-American law. I mean, they gave up habeas corpus. Simply redefine someone as an [unlawful] enemy combatant; that means they have no rights. And essentially anyone in the world who's suspected of terrorism can be arrested anyplace in the world, brought to an undisclosed place without a charge, and kept there indefinitely. There are people in Guantánamo who have been there for seven years with no charges against them except that they're "suspected of terrorism."

For me, it's not that the administration was "trapped in the situation." I'm saying they *created* the situation. They created a system in which each of these parts fall out. I'm saying they're responsible.

TS: In that expressive sense?

PZ: I like that expressive view, yes. But you know, if we were to be the losers of the war on terrorism, they would be brought before a war crimes tribunal. If there was in fact a real war, and we lost in Iraq, the Iraqis would say, "Okay, you invaded our country under false pretenses, you did all these things, all these people died. We're going to put you on trial."

VII. HEROES IN WAITING

TS: Let's conclude, as you do in your book, on a more optimistic note. You talk in your book about some ways to avoid some of the problems of succumbing to the situation. Knowing the power of the situation can help us resist when we ought to.

PZ: Yes.

TS: But I'm wondering how that's supposed to work in practice. Take the Asch conformity experiments.[8] It seems that the subjects

---

[8] In these studies, a subject was asked to evaluate the length of lines in the presence of other "subjects" who were really in collaboration with the investigators. When these "subjects" unan-

there are operating with this heuristic: "If everyone else is perceiving something, and I don't have any reason to think they're lying, then they're probably right and I'm wrong." Under normal circumstances, that seems pretty reasonable. How are we supposed to know when a situation is corrupting or illusory?

PZ: That's a good point. You said it right. Our life is organized around a bunch of heuristics to say "Under ordinary circumstances, when the majority of people see something a certain way, it's probably the way to see it." And in fact, in the real world, more often than not it is that way. Similarly, the majority of times when an authority says, "Here's what I believe, and here's what you should do," and you do it, it's for your advantage. Your parents, the priest, your teachers, the rabbi. The problem is that we aren't really taught to be sensitive to the exceptions to the rule. That is, parents abuse kids, priests abuse kids, authorities are sometimes false authorities, authorities are sometimes evil. In the Milgram study, it's all about somebody who starts off being a totally just authority and transforms to become totally unjust. At some point, they'd say: "I don't care if the guy has a heart attack, I don't care if he's dead in there. You have to keep shocking." At that point, you're an adult, and you should say "This doesn't make sense." Except that you've been so conditioned to be obedient to authority.

It's like the elementary school teacher who didn't let you get out of your seat unless you raised your hand to go to the toilet. And it didn't matter if you peed in your pants. I still remember in first grade, a little girl raised her hand and said, "I have to go to the bathroom." The teacher said, "No, put your hand down." The kid peed all over herself. Everyone laughed at her. We carry these sets of heuristics and we never get trained to be wary of the exception to the rule. Because that's where the danger lies. Sometimes the majority is wrong. In Nazi Germany, the majority was wrong to say, "We gotta kill Jews." In Rwanda, the majority among the Hu-

---

imously gave obviously wrong answers, the real subject started to give that answer as well, conforming with the rest of the group.

tus were wrong to say, "We gotta kill Tutsis." But that's the hardest thing. How do you, as an individual, become situationally savvy enough to say, "Wait, this situation is the exception"?

TS: Exactly. What should we do?

PZ: Part of it is having a certain level of skepticism, of cynicism, in the back of your optimism. So optimism is "I love the world, I love most people," but if I grew up in the ghetto, I developed street smarts, street savvy, which means I'm never fully trusting. I never trust anybody 100 percent. The Mafia thing. You always sit with your back to the wall. Nobody's ever going to come and take you from behind. Whenever you walk into a situation, the first thing you do is look for the exits, because you know if there's a fire, everybody's going to go to the exit they came in through, and you'll be crushed. And you're going to walk out the other one. It should be part of our basic training of being situationally sensitive, situationally savvy.

TS: Basic training at the parental level or the school level?

PZ: The school level, because again, most people are good most of the time, but there's always a bad apple. There's always the bully in the class. There's always the hustler. There's always the wheeler-dealer. There's always the pimp who's trying to get women to do what he wants.

TS: You can always stumble in a bad barrel.

PZ: Yeah, you can just make the wrong turn. And then you're in this bad thing. The terrible thing is by accident of birth. People grow up in inner cities, people grow up in war zones, people grow up in places where there's 200 percent inflation. And their lives are going to be powerfully impacted by those situations. But we still want to believe that they have individual freedom of choice to rise above it. And the interesting thing is, some few do. Most of them don't. If a guy gets released from prison and goes back to the neighborhood he came from, the chances of him having recidivism are enormous. If you put him in a different situation, give him a place to live, give him a job... They do this here, something called the Delancey Street Foundation. Instead of going to prison, they give you a job and an apartment immediately. And there's social support. They never break the law again. I don't know what the recidivism rate is, but it's probably 10 percent. It's as simple as that. If I have a job, if I have respect, and I have a place to live that's away from the bad situation, then I can exercise free choice and I can be a good person.

TS: So, in your skeptical sort of way, you think we can rise above our situations, or at least create situations which allow us to rise above bad ones?

PZ: My argument is in fact that most people are good most of the time. But evil makes the news. Evil is dramatic, evil is swift. So some kid spends hours making a sand castle and another kid comes and steps on it in a second and destroys it. Somebody spends years making a sculpture and someone comes with a hammer and breaks the arm off. So evil, graffiti, and all these kinds of things—destruction— are swift and powerful. If it bleeds, it leads. All the news organizations, they want the stories about evil. They want the death and the violence, the incest and the rape. I'm saying most people, most of the time, don't do anything bad. Maybe they cheat on their income tax and feel guilty about it. The last chapter of my book is not only about how you resist, it's also a celebration of heroism as the real antidote to evil. And that's the main thing I'm doing now. I'm starting the Heroic Imagination Project. To be consistent, I say most evil is done by ordinary people put in certain situations. And it's the *act* that's really evil—most people are really not. Most heroes, most heroic acts, are also done by ordinary people who aren't special in any way. They just happen to be put into a certain situation of emergency, of evil, of immorality, of corruption, that gives them the opportunity to act on it.

TS: Joe Darby, the Abu Ghraib whistle-blower, for example. You discuss him in your book.

PZ: Yes. Most heroes are ordinary people put in a situation, often only once in their lifetime, that gives them the opportunity to act. So what I've been trying to do has been to democratize heroism and demystify it. There're two kind of heroes. There are impulsive heroes, and there are reflective heroes—people who blow the whistle on Enron. Sherron Watkins and others. Christians who helped the Jews. But what I'm saying—Gandhi, Nelson Mandela, Martin Luther King Jr., Mother Teresa, they're exceptional. The reason we know their names is that they organized their whole lives around a sacrifice. And it's great that they did it. I'm not gonna do it, I'm not going to give up my whole life to any cause. But in fact, I think Obama said his grandmother was the unsung hero. Most people who do heroic things, sacrifice for others, they do it in silence. Every single person who's identified as a hero always says, "How could I not do it?"

TS: So there's the banality of evil and the "banality of heroism."

PZ: The banality of heroism. I think that's a reasonable expression, and it really says that it's the heroic act that's extraordinary because it's rare. And so if we can have more and more kids think, "I'm a hero in waiting," and if we can have hero resources in schools and summer camps where kids learn situational savvy, these kinds of street smarts, they can learn social influence skills to form a network. So you want them to say, "I'm a hero in waiting," and then "I have to be prepared. I have to learn first-aid skills, I have to learn social influence skills, I have to learn a set of things, and that when the time comes, I will act!" ✳

PART II

WHERE DID MORALITY COME FROM? WHAT IS IT? WHERE IS IT GOING?

Why are we moral, anyway? Why do we give anonymously to charity, and get a nice warm fuzzy feeling when we do it? Why do we feel guilty when we break promises or cheat friends and even strangers? Why do we think it's morally appalling to walk by a child drowning in a pond, but okay to buy big-screen TVs when that money could buy mosquito nets that would save the lives of African children? These are just a few of the questions that the researchers in this section attempt to answer.

In Chapter 3, primatologist Frans de Waal explains how moral attitudes and feelings like empathy are deeply rooted in our evolutionary history, tracing back to before our split with other primates like chimpanzees and bonobos. Next, the philosopher of biology Michael Ruse explores the philosophical implications of a Darwinian account of morality. In Chapter 5, anthropologist Joe Henrich discusses his work in Fiji and the Peruvian Amazon on the cross-cultural differences and similarities in beliefs about justice. Finally, neuroscientists Joshua Greene and Liane Young discuss their groundbreaking research using functional MRI machines to investigate the neuroscience behind moral judgment.

Some might find this research and its conclusions unsettling. We're only moral because moral feelings helped our primate and hominid ancestors leave more offspring? Right and wrong can depend on where you live? That's not morality! Maybe *this* curtain should stay closed. But the story of how and why we are moral is too fascinating and complex for this pessimism to be sustained. Uncovering the origins and mechanisms behind human morality need not diminish the central role it plays in our lives.

3

FRANS DE WAAL

LESSONS FROM OUR PRIMATE RELATIVES

Two elephants walk together at night. (No, this isn't a joke—it's a scene from a wildlife reserve in Thailand.) There is heavy rain, and the older elephant slips and falls in the mud. She's unable to get up. The younger elephant, unrelated to her companion, stays beside her for most of the night. The next day a group of mahouts, elephant caretakers from the wildlife reserve, try to hoist the elephant up to her feet with braces and ropes. In all the commotion—a crowd has gathered to watch the rescue—the younger elephant remains by the side of her fallen friend. The mahouts and the crowd shout for her to move out of the way, so they can get better leverage. But she won't budge. Instead, she burrows her head under the body of the other elephant and tries to lift her up. She does this several times, risking injury in the attempts. Incredibly, the younger elephant appears to recognize that the mahouts want to help rather than hurt her friend. She times her pushes, or so it seemed to me, with the hoisting of the mahouts.

Until recently, biologists thought such complex behavior—behavior with an undeniable moral dimension—was exclusive to human beings. As much as anyone in the world, the primatologist Frans de Waal is responsible for changing this perception. Starting with Chimpanzee Politics—his fascinating account of the intrigues and machinations of a chimpanzee troupe in the Arnhem Zoo[1]—and continuing through more recent books like *Good Natured* and *Our Inner Ape,* de Waal has illustrated the uncanny similarities between human beings and our primate relatives. De Waal has not restricted himself to descriptions of behavior, however. He is famous for his willingness to enter into the largely taboo world of animal emotions, where research is routinely dismissed as "anthropomorphizing." The result is an impressive array of evidence suggesting that we are not the only species to have moral feelings.

De Waal's research is no friend to human vanity. In the grand tradition of Galileo and Darwin, de Waal provokes those who seek to draw a clear line between human beings and everything else. But his message is an optimistic one. If human morality has deep roots in our evolutionary past, then we can expect it to be more resilient, less susceptible to the contingencies of history. Seeing morality in this light also undermines the view of human beings as inherently selfish—a view that de Waal terms "veneer theory." Morality, according to this theory, is merely a recent cultural invention, a thin veneer that masks our "true" selfish animal nature. De Waal's criticisms of this theory (which we discuss at some length below) are the topic of his most recent book, *Primates and Philosophers.* The book is based on lectures de Waal presented at Princeton Univer-

---

[1] De Waal was approached by television producers about making a reality TV show based on this book. The show would document the behavior and strategies of two groups under similar conditions—one made up of chimpanzees, the other made up of humans. De Waal declined after learning that the producers wanted him to stage some of the behavior of the chimpanzees.

sity, and features responses to his work from four renowned philosophers and authors.

De Waal is also a remarkably hospitable interview subject. When I arrived in the morning, I was treated to a tour of the primate center and a bucket of apples to throw to the chimps in their enclosures. (There are very few things I'd rather do than toss apples to chimpanzees.) After the interview, Josh Plotkin,[2] one of de Waal's graduate students, showed me videos of his work in Thailand—including the video depicting the elephant rescue attempt described above. That evening, I was invited to de Waal's house for a dinner highlighted by hitchhiking stories from his wife, Catherine, and capped with a shot of "the cognac of tequilas." The interview itself took place at the Yerkes National Primate Research Center, about forty minutes north of Atlanta.

January 2007

I. BONOBOS GONE WILD

TAMLER SOMMERS: I want to discuss your work with chimpanzees especially, but let's start by talking about the bonobos, the closest primate relative of the chimpanzee. Your accounts of bonobos have always been great reading. You call them the "hippie ape," you describe some of their interactions as "orgies"—the reader gets a general sense of them as a sort of nonviolent free-love egalitarian noble-savage kind of animal. You'd think they'd be the celebrities of the animal kingdom. Instead, they are, in your words, "the forgotten ape." Why have they been forgotten?

FRANS DE WAAL: Well, first of all, we've only recently learned about the bonobos. The first discovery of these types of apes was the chimpanzee, whom Europeans have known since the seventeenth century. And even the few bonobos we did know then were called chimpanzees—everything was a chimpanzee at the time. So

---

[2] Josh has recently become well-known in the popular press for leading the first study (with de Waal) to demonstrate that elephants can recognize themselves in mirrors.

that's one reason they were discovered much later. The fieldwork was done much later. There were very few captive studies. The other reason is that the story of the bonobo didn't fit the thinking.

TS: Which thinking is that?

FDW: The postwar thinking was that we're an aggressive species. Which is pretty logical after World War II. But it became a kind of obsession to ask: Why are we so aggressive? Is it an instinct or is it not an instinct? Is it ingrained in our natures or not? That was the issue. One camp, mostly biologists, claimed that we were by nature aggressive. And a group of anthropologists used the chimpanzee initially as a counterexample. These anthropologists said, "Look at the ape. Our close relatives just travel through the trees and eat fruit and are peaceful. So that means that our ancestors were probably peaceful and aggression is a cultural product."

TS: Probably a comforting thought.

FDW: Yes, but in the '70s, when the first reports came out about chimpanzees killing each other and killing monkeys, all of a sudden the counterarguments to the biologists were wiped off the table. And people saw this as the ultimate proof that human beings are an aggressive, nasty, and selfish species. The chimpanzee became the primary model for the human species and everything just clicked into place. That was the new model: "We are aggressive, they are aggressive, we must have been aggressive for six million years. Look at the ape."

TS: And then came the bonobos.

FDW: Yes, then along came the behavioral data on bonobos in the '80s. And they didn't fit into the *new* picture. And they still don't fit into that picture. And so there are still people who will argue that the last common ancestor for humans was more chimplike. But there's no good argument for that. Genetically, they are exactly equidistant to us as they are to the chimpanzee. There's no good reason except for an ideological reason. They don't fit the new thinking about the inherent aggressiveness of human beings.

TS: They fit the previous thinking.

FDW: Yes. Basically, if your view is that human beings are an inherently aggressive species, then the bonobo is problematic. If your view is that humans have all sorts of characteristics including being highly cooperative, then the bonobos are a very interesting example to look at. I take the position that I don't know which one better reflects our own nature. I think we have a lot of both.

TS: Can you describe some of the ways bonobos break out of the warmongering mold?

FDW: First, there is no evidence from the field or from studies in captivity that bonobos kill each other. This has been seen many times in chimpanzees: killing each other, killing infants. For bonobos this has never been seen. They are friendlier, more peaceful. It's not that they are never aggressive; they are. But they don't kill. And they have a very effective way of avoiding aggression, which is their sexual interactions. So that's one issue. And the other is that female bonobos collectively dominate the males, which probably also helps control aggression. So it's a female-dominated species, and a very sexy species, none of which fits the thinking of mostly male theoreticians.

TS: You tell a funny story in *Our Inner Ape* about a lecture in which you described the failure of male bonobos to fight and establish dominance over the females. An audience member raised his hand and asked: "Well, what's *wrong* with them? What's wrong with these male bonobos?"

FDW: Right. Many male scientists react that way. Bonobos are uncomfortable to have around. They're too peaceful, and they're female-dominated. We can't handle that. Now, I personally don't think that our ancestors were female-dominated. That developed for the bonobo. But even if our last common ancestor was female-dominated, that would be very interesting. We would need a different evolutionary story to explain how we got where we are. I always feel that facts that are inconvenient for certain theories should be faced straight-on rather than be neglected.

TS: I like what you said in one of the books—that the male bonobos have it pretty good. They're sexually liberated, they have a low-stress existence...

FDW: There's objective evidence for that. Most groups of chimpanzees have twice as many adult females as males. Most groups of bonobos have equal numbers of adult males and females. Since the birth ratio is fifty-fifty for both species, there must be a lot of male chimpanzees who die early. And that probably has to do with all the fighting and tensions and stress levels and so on. So in terms of health and longevity the male bonobo has a better life than the chimpanzee male.

TS: I have to bring up "GG-rubbing." My wife and I have *The Forgotten Ape* on a table in our living room, and any time we have a party, if it's a good party, anyway, someone will start flipping through the book and showing everyone the pictures of the female bonobos GG-rubbing.

FDW: [*Laughing*] Is that right? Like having *Playboy* on the coffee table.

TS: Right, *Primate Playboy*. Something about the act, the name—it's a great name, *GG-rubbing*. And the picture. It demands attention. What is GG-rubbing, exactly? And what is its purpose? Why do female bonobos engage in it so often?

FDW: GG-rubbing is when females cling to each other almost like mother and child, and they rub their genitals together—basically a sexual interaction. In the US there's a shyness about sex, as you probably know, so many people who work on bonobos in this country don't want to call it sex. So they would say it's "affiliation" or it's "friendly"—

TS: It seems extremely friendly.

FDW: —or they'll say it's not sex because it's not reproductive, which excludes, I suppose, all gay sex as sex. In fact, I thought it was amusing when the Paula Jones case came along in the US, that they actually had to find a definition of sex. Because Clinton tried to deny that he had sex with someone, and so the court came up with a definition—and they said sex is all contact involving the genitals. So it's official now: GG-rubbing has officially been declared sex. I use that argument if anyone wants to call it something else. And it clearly is sex. They rub their genitals and their clitorises together. Partly it resolves conflicts between them. Partly it's a conciliatory thing. It's a greeting. Mostly it promotes bonding between them. And the bonding is a very strong political instrument, because female bonobos only dominate the males collectively. A female is not individually capable of dominating a male. So GG-rubbing is basically a political tool.

II. THE REAL DARWINIAN POSITION

TS: Much of your work recently has been aimed at correcting another misconception—that morality is exclusively a human invention, something that evolved long after we split from other apes. Do you think apes and bonobos are moral species? Do they exhibit moral behavior?

FDW: Well, I usually don't call it moral behavior. I tend to call it building blocks or *prerequisites* for morality. I don't think that chimpanzees are moral beings in the human sense. But they do have empathy, sympathy, reciprocity. They share food, resolve conflicts. All of these elements are present in human morality. So what I argue is that the basic psychology of the great apes is an essential *element* of human morality. Humans add things to that, making our morality far more complex. And that's why I don't want to call chimpanzees moral beings, exactly.

TS: Why do you want to hesitate if you believe that chimpanzees have gratitude and empathy, indignation, maybe—what we call the moral emotions?

FDW: They have the moral emotions, yes. You can see gratitude, outrage, a sense of fairness—you can see parallels and equivalences in all the great apes. But to get to morality you need more than just the emotions. So yes, empathy is a good thing to have. And I cannot imagine how humans could have morality without empathy, but what morality adds to that, for example, is what Adam Smith termed the "impartial spectator." You need to be able to look at a situation and make a judgment about that situation even though it doesn't affect you yourself. So I can see an interaction between two humans and say this one is wrong and this one is right. I'm not convinced that chimpanzees have this kind of distance in their judgments. They certainly have judgments about what they do and how they interact with others. And how others treat them. I'm sure they have opinions about specific social interactions and how to react to them, but do they have opinions about more abstract interactions around them and a concept about what kind of society they want to live in? Do they have a concept about fairness between others, or do they only care about fairness for themselves? That kind of distance that you see in human moral reasoning. I'm not sure you'll find that in a chimpanzee.

TS: Correct me if I'm wrong, but I thought I read something in *Chimpanzee Politics* and some other work indicating that chimps do react with a kind of indignation when they see one chimp mistreating another chimp. A third party will react, punishing the offender.

FDW: Yes, true. Yes.

TS: Wouldn't that count?

FDW: Yes—I think you can probably find examples of this in chimpanzee life. But in a way, even the interactions around them affect themselves: these are their friends, their relatives, their rivals. They are never impartial spectators. If chimpanzees have a morality, it likely is a self-centered morality.

TS: Can you give some examples of empathy in other species?

FDW: Well, yes. Today, you saw that old [chimpanzee] female Penny, who can barely get up on the climb bars, right?

TS: Yes.

FDW: We often see young females push her up onto the climber. So that's altruistic helping because it's really hard to imagine that they're doing it to get some favor back from this old lady. I give many examples in my books of sophisticated empathetic behavior in chimpanzees, including those that clearly require "theory of mind"—the ability to take the perspective of other chimps.

TS: So you think when a young chimp is helping Penny up the climb bars, she feels her frustration in some way, and she does this by taking her perspective, imagining what it must be like not to be able to climb on her own?

FDW: Well, the young chimp must understand Penny's goal and also the trouble she has trying to reach her goal. That's a very complex action right there. In humans there is a literature that says that perspective-taking requires a strong sense of self. A "self-other" distinction. Which is why in children, perspective-taking comes only at two years, when they are able to recognize themselves in the mirror. So we did the mirror-recognition experiments with chimps and also recently with elephants. Because elephants are very well known as highly altruistic animals. And they have large brains. So the thinking was that more complex empathy, based on perspective-taking, must correlate with mirror recognition.

TS: I saw Yale biologist Laurie Santos give a talk on perspective-taking or "theory of mind" capacities in monkeys, and I was amazed by the question-answer period. Hands shot up—everyone tried to come up with alternate explanations for her findings, even ones that were ad hoc to a bizarre degree. There was such deep skepticism, which was surprising from an outsider's perspective. From my point of view, I thought, Of *course* other animals can take the perspective of others; of *course* they can imagine what other monkeys or chimps are thinking or feeling. But obviously that's not the common view among biologists.

FDW: It's a recent bias. Previous experiments showed that chimpanzees had this ability, and in that period—this was in the '70s—the findings didn't get much attention. No one cared. Then a bunch of studies came along in the '80s that cast doubt on those findings. And then everyone jumped on those studies and said: "There it is! Now we have the big difference between humans and animals—'theory of mind,' taking the perspective of others. That's what distinguishes us." I think that people are extremely eager to find that kind of difference. There's a long history, going all the way back to Darwin, before Darwin, where certain small items were believed to be uniquely human features. At one time there was thought to be a small bone in our jaw that was only human, but then they found it in other species. The ability to use tools was a big one, until Jane Goodall discovered tool-use by chimpanzees in the field. Then language. And recently theory of mind became the big thing. But now, of course, it's crumbling. There are more and more findings coming out that perspective-taking is not even restricted to primates—probably dogs have it, some birds may have it.

TS: Dogs have it? I knew it!

FDW: Yes, there are good findings on dogs, ravens, goats. At some level or other, perspective-taking is present in many animals. It may reach its highest level in big-brained animals—dolphins, elephants, chimpanzees, and I'm sure humans go beyond this... but it's a continuum. We're farther along on the continuum, but it's not completely absent in other animals. And that's upsetting to a lot of people.

TS: Meanwhile, your most recent book, *Primates and Philosophers,* attacks the view that *human beings* aren't really moral, never mind nonhumans. You argue against the view that human morality is a thin veneer, a kind of cultural overlay or hypocritical mask covering our deeply selfish animal nature. You see this as fundamentally misguided because of the connection between our morality and animal emotions.

FDW: The interesting thing about my position is that it's really the old Darwinian position: human morality is an outflow of primate sociality. That's how Darwin saw it—it's an outgrowth of the social instincts. It's also very close to a Humean position and to Adam Smith. It's a moral sentimentalism—the view that emotions drive morality. In the last thirty years, people have abandoned that view. Richard Dawkins; Robert Wright in *The Moral Animal;* Michael Ghiselin; T. H. Huxley, a contemporary of Darwin's. They all take this position that evolution could never have produced morality, because evolution produces only selfish, nasty, aggressive individuals. And obviously human morality is a way of going beyond that. So evolution could not have produced human morality—it is something *we* came up with. What annoys me is that this is being sold as a *Darwinian* position. As if the true Darwinian paradigm dictates that evolution cannot have produced morality. But if you read Darwin's book *The Descent of Man,* it's very obvious that Darwin himself did not agree with this view at all.

So we've been fed a bogus "Darwinian" position for thirty years, one that confuses the way evolution works with the things that evolution produces. Because the way evolution works, yes—it's a nasty process. Evolution works by eliminating those who are not successful. Natural selection is a process that cares only about your own reproduction, or gene replication, and everything else is irrelevant. But then what natural selection *produces* is extremely variable. Natural selection can produce the social indifference you find in many solitary animals. But it can also produce extremely cooperative, friendly, and empathic characteristics. But this product of natural selection is ignored. And so, for example, human empathy is often presented as some sort of afterthought of evolution or something contrived—some people have argued that we are never *truly* empathic and kind. But if you look at the neuroscience literature on human empathy, it's obvious that it's an automated reaction. That's a strong counterargument to the claim that empathy is a contrived, culturally influenced trait. Because people cannot even suppress empathy. So take, for example, people in a movie theater where something terrible is about to happen. What do people do?

TS: They slam their hands over their eyes.

FDW: Yes. The reason we do that is that empathy is such a strong reaction, we have no control over it, and the only way to get control over it is to block the images. So I think empathy is a deeply seated characteristic of the human species. And it's by no means limited to the human species; it's a very old mammalian characteristic. Recently a paper came up on mice empathy. So it's a very ancient characteristic which fits with Darwin's position and my position on empathy and its origin. In *Good Natured* and *Primates and Philosophers,* I take a stand that this whole line of thinking is confused—the line of thinking that says by nature we're nasty and so we can never *naturally* get to morality. It's not that I don't think culture influences human morality. I do think that. But certainly we didn't start from scratch when we evolved morality.

TS: We started with moral emotions—which are as much a part of our natures as the selfish drives we have.

FDW: Absolutely.

TS: In your book you say that the "veneer theory" is a result of something you call "Beethoven's error." Can you explain what that is?

FDW: Beethoven's error is the confusion I alluded to between process and outcome. The focus on the process of natural selection started in the '70s with Dawkins, who popularized the view that selection occurred at the level of the gene. This took us to the bare minimum and everyone focused all the attention on the selection process. But if you do that, you forget about the beautiful things that the process can produce. People like Dawkins focused their whole mind on the *nastiness* of the selection process. And they were intent on providing a sort of shock therapy to people in the social sciences and philosophy. And when the social scientists would say, "But sometimes people are kind to each other," they would reply, "No, no, that's all made up, they're faking that. There has to be some sort of selfish ulterior motive behind it." And so I called this type of error the "Beethoven error" because Beethoven produced his most beautiful music under the most atrocious circumstances (his Vienna apartment was described as disorganized and incredibly dirty). And that's true for a lot of process/outcome errors. Take cooking. The process of cooking is by no means clean and attractive. If you go into a Chinese restaurant's kitchen, you probably don't want to eat Chinese for a while. But you *do* eat it because we make that distinction. We forget about the process and enjoy the product. Natural selection produces some beautiful things—like genuine empathy.

III. "HUMAN CARING IS PREDICATED ON AFFORDABILITY."

TS: On to a more philosophical topic. You seem to believe we can learn some moral lessons from the behavior of other nonhuman primates today. How does that work? What can the behavior of chimpanzees and other primates teach us about our own behavior?

How can we derive claims about how we ought to act?

FDW: I'm not sure we can directly derive it.

TS: Well, okay—how can primate research *influence* the way we want to guide our behavior or design our institutions?

FDW: If you start from the assumption that humans are entirely competitive and that everything is regulated by selfish motives— and Americans do this more than Europeans—you end up with the conservative streak which is largely based on this kind of social Darwinist idea: let people fend for themselves, they will ultimately improve themselves or they'll die off, which is also fine. That sort of very harsh political ideology is often sold as being *congruent* with how nature operates. You look at free-market capitalism as an extension of nature. Wall Street is a Darwinian jungle. But this is not how human nature actually operates. People are not completely guided by selfish motives. A lot of work coming out of behavioral economics challenges this view that humans act selfishly even in *economic* life, never mind social life. Even economic decision-making is not driven exclusively by selfish motives. And social life, social considerations, and behavior are even less purely tied to selfish drives. A full understanding of human nature, helped by an understanding of the nature of our closest primates, will very quickly lead you to the conclusion, as Adam Smith well understood, that free-market capitalism needs to be counterbalanced by social motives. And then you'll get more of a mitigated type of capitalism, a softer capitalism. That doesn't mean you eliminate the free market. But it means that you build a society in which there is care for the poor, where there is reciprocity for others.

TS: But I'm still not clear on how you "get" that mitigated capitalism...

FDW: Take Hurricane Katrina, for example, which in the US exposed the line of thinking that we don't need to care about the poor, that they will fend for themselves. So then the biggest disaster of the century comes and the poor are left behind. All of a sudden, the American people were very embarrassed about what happened. All of a sudden, people were embarrassed by the fact that they didn't really care about the poor—that they had just let them drown. Most people had fled the city, leaving the old, sick, and poor behind. The people who couldn't move in to the hospitals were just left behind. This was an interesting moment in American history, because all of a sudden it exposed this line of thinking as not compatible with how we *want* to be. And in fact it's not compatible with how we are as a species.

TS: But when you say that a true understanding of human nature gets us a softer mitigated capitalism, that leads me to believe that if the social Darwinians were right about the inherent selfishness of human beings, they would have been justified in setting up a hard, ruthless capitalism. Do you believe that?

FDW: Imagine that we were exactly as described by social Darwinists or Republicans—selfish, 100 percent incentive-driven, that's all. Then there would really be no reason to change society. We could go full-blown toward capitalism and a free market and see what happens.

TS: You really think there would be no reason to resist this even if we *were* primarily driven by selfish motives? Isn't it possible that we should care for others just because we think it's the right thing to do, even though we may not want to do it?

FDW: You think that people will do things that are right, even if they don't want to?

TS: They might… we don't always do what we want to do.

FDW: I don't think that people will do that. The fact that the American people were embarrassed by Katrina, or that a large proportion of the American people want improved health care, or to care for the poor, is I think purely because there is a level of empathy. You need to indoctrinate empathy *out* of people in order to arrive at extreme capitalist positions. And those people who will publicly argue that we don't need to care about the poor, they will care privately, if they have a poor family member, they will take care of that family member. So it's only *other* poor people they don't care about.

TS: Of course; it's still *their* family, right? As you note, the dark side of our nature is that we favor the interests of our "in-group," especially the family, although that can be broadened a little. But the farther that goes, the less we care about others, and the more we're willing to act violently toward them and neglect them.

FDW: I think that human morality evolved as an in-group phenomenon, to strengthen the in-group and increase its cohesiveness. This was partly needed for competition with other groups. So what you did to the other groups didn't matter. You could hack them to pieces, that would be perfectly fine, as long as you didn't hack *each other* to pieces—within the in-group. And that's a really interesting thing. The worst side of human nature, which is really intergroup violence between religions and between ethnic groups or nations, this side is *also* linked to the evolution of morality. And that's also why if people now argue that we need to expand morality and have universal human rights, and that we need to care about people elsewhere in the world, they have a big challenge ahead of them.

TS: Can primate research help them take this into account—help them see that we're not built for caring about people with whom have no connection with at all?

FDW: Of course, I'm not saying we *shouldn't* care. I don't think primate research offers that kind of moral guideline. All I'm saying is that it will be a challenge. I think as soon as we lose our wealth, the caring we do have for distant out-groups will disappear. Given that we are wealthy as a nation, in that sense, we ought to care about others. But as soon as there's a crash in our economy, like in the '20s, say, something really serious,[3] will we still care about distant people? Human caring is predicated on affordability. Moral obligations to the out-group are not—however much philosophers might wish them to be so[4]—independent of moral obligations to the in-group. Our first priority is the survival of ourselves and our close kin. I call this the role of loyalty: we have varying degrees of loyalty, and they are just not equal for distant and close people, or for humans and animals, for that matter.

TS: You also say that we have a mental switch that when triggered can turn friend into foe. An attack of some kind can trigger this. You said that our reaction to Iraq is perhaps an example of this kind of primitive impulse that you see even in chimpanzees.

FDW: If you hit yourself with a hammer, you're going to blame someone—anyone. Frustration leads to angry reactions. This is known as the scapegoat effect, which occurs even in rats. You place two rats on an electric grid and shock them: they will attack each other as if the other is to blame for the pain. In primates, we often see that if there are tensions among higher-ups, they pick on a low-ranking individual to attack it. I felt the same happened in the United States after 9/11. A big and mighty country got attacked on its own soil—something it's not used to—and so someone had to be blamed, someone had to be attacked to let off steam. The target's actual guilt was a secondary concern. Afghanistan was not big enough for the angry reaction the US wanted to show. What struck me most was the cheerleading in the media. At the moment, everyone is backtracking and questioning the wisdom of the attack, but at the time it happened, all I saw was great enthusiasm. As a result, what is it, five hundred thousand Iraqis are gone? It's a disaster.

---

[3] This interview, of course, took place in early 2007.

[4] De Waal is almost certainly referring to Peter Singer here. See Singer's interview with Sahar Akhtar in the February 2006 issue of the *Believer*. Singer is one of the authors that responds to de Waal in *Primates and Philosophers*.

IV. "GOOD OLD PRIMATE DIPLOMACY"

TS: Why do you think chimpanzees and bonobos have such different types of existences? They're such close relatives, genetically speaking, and yet violence and aggression are so common in one species, and harmony and GG-rubbing are so common in the other. What accounts for that difference?

FDW: Well, the leading theory is that bonobos live in a richer environment. They have the whole forest for themselves; they don't share it with gorillas. (Whereas chimpanzees are in competition with gorillas.) And this permits female bonobos to travel together. Chimpanzee females do not have that same opportunity because in order to gather food they have to travel separately. Oddly enough, that could be the reason for everything. Because if the females can travel together, they can form bonds and coalitions, and a lot of things like female dominance can follow from there.

TS: Is there a lesson we can draw from their environmental differences? Should we encourage a kind of society where women can travel together, and with their children—which might lead to a less-aggressive dynamic? Or are other social, environmental, behavioral differences too great for this to work...

FDW: That's the problem. We have such a different past in terms of family building. We are in a situation where the nuclear family is so important, which bonobos don't have. So I'm not sure how from there you get to some kind of bonobo society where everybody mates with everybody. We have been subject to different evolutionary pressures, which is very difficult to return from.

TS: Would it be a fool's errand to try?

FDW: I think so. We have a social system where there is male investment in offspring. That always means that you get a protection of the investment. So males have reasons to develop social systems and moral systems that protect the family—emphasizing virginity, emphasizing fidelity, at least for the women, not necessarily for the men, but certainly for the women. Our society is designed around that system. So if we were to move in the direction of the bonobos, we would destroy that system. And that would create other serious problems. The funny thing is that many people look at bonobos as a kind of paragon, the type of situation we want to have—egalitarian relationships, free sex, peaceful. It all sounds very wonderful, but I don't think it's an option given where we are now.

TS: But on the other hand, you do seem to think there's a lot of cultural variability within our own species. Yes, the genes "hold culture on a leash," as E.O. Wilson said, but how long is the leash? And how much control do we have over where we go when attached to it?

FDW: There are certain cultures that emphasize harmony. For example, the Japanese culture emphasizes getting along in a way that American culture does not. The emphasis here is more that you have to stick up for yourself—don't get beaten up by anyone. Beat them up. It's a very different attitude. I don't know what triggers a society to move in one direction rather than another direction. But I'm a primatologist, not a sociologist.

TS: But you haven't been shy, though, about imagining ways in which the theories and themes from your work might affect social policy for human beings.

FDW: Well, the only thing I can say is that you will find people (or animals) being more cooperative with each other if you emphasize shared interest. And that's what, for example, Japanese society does. In this society, you could emphasize shared interest or group interest more, that would be the way to do it. Instead of saying something like "You shouldn't fight!"

TS: So do you think that you've learned things as a primatologist that can be applied to human problems? Or is that not something that really interests you?

FDW: No, it is of interest. Because, for example, in the US there are many conflict-resolution programs at schools. They basically tell kids to shake hands after fights and say, "I'm sorry." That's not going to do *anything* to resolve the real conflict. Of course kids are smart enough to learn that that's what the teacher wants, so that's what they're going to do. But you're not changing the *attitudes.* What you need to do is teach them that there is value in relationships or value to the group and then the rest will follow. There will be fewer fights, less conflict. And there are great social psychology experiments to back this up. If you create competition between groups, you'll find higher social cohesiveness within the groups. The same thing happens to nations. A nation at war, like the US was a couple of years ago, is a more cohesive nation. So those kinds of lessons to me are pretty obvious.

TS: This reminds me of your discussion of sex differences too. One of the things you talk about is how males—and you see this in humans and chimpanzees—will fight more often, but they are much better at conflict resolution. Whereas females don't fight as often, but when they do, it's for keeps. There's no resolution.

FDW: That's sometimes controversial, because people always assume women are more peaceful than men. Which in many senses is true. Look at the murder rate. But I do believe that women are not nearly as good at conflict resolution, and that's why they try much harder to avoid conflict. And they're often successful. But when the conflict surfaces....

TS: Women hold grudges.

FDW: Yes, often there is no resolution. A lot of women, especially intellectual women, can't stand that idea. They've grown up on the view that women are good and men are bad. What men do is compete and fight—and that's all they can do. But it's actually, who was it, Golda Meir, I don't know, a female politician said something to the effect that "It's good that men wage war, because it's only men who can make peace."

TS: In other words, Obama '08?

FDW: Remember, I'm not voting.[5] But if you want my opinion, what the US needs most at this point is a leader who understands that this country, however important, has only 5 percent of the world population. You're as much caught in the web of international affairs and global economy as anyone else, so instead of trying to play the bully—without much success, I might add—you'd be better off with good old primate diplomacy. What you need is a groomer-in-chief. ✸

---

[5] De Waal is a Dutch citizen.

4

MICHAEL RUSE

THE ILLUSION OF OBJECTIVITY

We all have strong moral beliefs and make confident moral judgments. Terrorists are evil; discrimination is wrong. But where do these beliefs come from? One answer is that there are moral facts out there in the world waiting to be discovered, and rational creatures like us are capable of discovering them. Another is that these moral beliefs are part of a specific human psychology that has developed during the course of evolutionary history. According to this view, the urge to help thy neighbor is a result of the same evolutionary process that produced the urge to sleep with thy neighbor's wife. Both urges are adaptations, like the human eye or the opposable thumb, and have evolved because they conferred higher fitness on the organisms that possessed them.

For more than thirty years, the philosopher Michael Ruse has championed this latter view. His 1986 book *Taking Darwin Seriously* is a full-length defense of the position that the theory of natural selection has a lot to tell us about our moral lives. Since then, Dr. Ruse—professor of philosophy at Florida State University and an absurdly prolific author—has written numerous books and articles clarifying and expanding his purely naturalistic approach to morality, religion, and epistemology. His most recent book is called *Darwinism and its Discontents.*

Ruse and other like-minded theorists have generated excitement with their views, and a fair amount of controversy as well. Criticism of evolutionary ethics is a bipartisan affair. From the left come attacks from a large and vocal contingent of academics, who range from being baffled to being appalled by the claim that human nature is not entirely a social construction. (The great evolutionary biologist and entomologist E. O. Wilson—coauthor of a number of articles with Ruse—was known to certain university activists as "the prophet of the right-wing patriarchy." During the course of one of Wilson's lectures, a group that called itself Science For the People dumped a bucket of ice water on his head and then chanted "You're all wet.") On the right, there are the hard-line moral realists engaged in their search for "moral clarity." To them, Darwinism introduces an element of subjectivity that threatens to undermine the certainty they bring to ethical affairs. And of course there are the religious fundamentalists, who object not only to a Darwinian approach to ethics but to the truth of evolutionary theory itself. Ruse got a taste of this brand of anti-Darwinian sentiment during his involvement in the infamous Arkansas creation trial of 1981. I began our interview—which took place over email and on the phone—by asking about this experience.

June 2003

I. OPEN BAR AT THE ACLU

TAMLER SOMMERS: In 1981, the state of Arkansas passed a law requiring science teachers who taught evolution to give equal time to something called "creation science." The ACLU sued the state, and you served as one of their expert witnesses. First of all, what exactly is creation science?

MICHAEL RUSE: Well, it's a form of American fundamentalism and biblical literalism. It's the belief that the Bible, particularly the early chapters of Genesis, are a reliable guide to history, including life history. Creationism itself is not a new phenomenon—it goes back certainly to the nineteenth century. The basic tenets are: the world is 6,000 years old, there was a miraculous creation, a universal flood, that sort of thing. Creation science as such is a phenomenon of the 1960s and '70s; it was polished up in order to get around the US Constitution's separation of church and state. And that's why they call it creation *science*. Because they want to claim scientifically that Genesis can be proven.

TS: What role did the ACLU want you to play in overturning the law?

MR: I was one of the expert witnesses called to testify against the law. Technically speaking, they were just trying to show that creation science is not science. So my job as a philosopher was to testify as to the nature of science and the nature of religion, and show that evolution is science, and creation science is religion.

TS: And so because of that, it did not deserve equal time in the classroom.

MR: It was not a question of what it deserves. The Constitution forbids the teaching of religion in publicly funded schools in America.

TS: In your book *But Is It Science?* you describe the trial, and you talk about the deposition you gave to the assistant attorney general of Arkansas, David Williams—it sounded like quite a grilling. At one point he asks you how you regard morality. You respond, "I intuit moral values as objective realities." Fortunately, you say, Williams didn't ask what you meant by that. But since it's relevant to the topic of this interview, what did you mean exactly?

MR: I'm not sure, really. I don't think of that as accurate, exactly, as to what my position really is. I think if you look at books that I wrote, like *Sociobiology: Sense or Nonsense?*, I certainly didn't think that morality could be reduced to evolutionary biology, in those days. I'm not sure if I've changed my mind, or come to a fuller understanding of the issue. I think I would still say that part of my position on morality is very much that we regard morality in some sense as being objective, even if it isn't. So the claim that we intuit morality as objective reality—I would still say that. Of course, what I would want to add is that from the fact that we do this, it doesn't follow that morality really is objective.

TS: I like your account of the "hospitality room" the afternoon before the trial. It was you, a bunch of religion witnesses, and an open bar. But they were witnesses for the ACLU, right?

MR: Yes, they were there to testify that it certainly isn't traditional religion to be forced to accept a literal reading of the Bible. Bruce Vawter, a Catholic priest, pointed out that if you go back to St. Augustine and earlier, they've all argued that one should be able to interpret the Bible metaphorically if science and the facts dictate otherwise, and so it follows that the Bible taken literally isn't necessarily true. The theologian Langdon Gilkey was arguing this, too, but from a contemporary theological perspective. Most theologians today, he said, do not believe in an absolutely literal interpretation of the Bible. And there was also George Marsden, an eminent historian who talked about the development of the fundamentalist movement and how it came into being. And again, trying to show very much that this is not traditional Christianity, but rather an indigenous form of American Protestant Christianity.

TS: But you say that the lawyers for the ACLU may have made a mistake in having an open bar right before the rehearsal.

MR: Well, I think they were worried that we'd all be sloshed or hung over before the actual trial. I mean, open bar... Well, we may have had a few gins, but it wasn't like a...

TS: Fraternity party.

MR: Or even a meeting of the APA.[1]

TS: So the rehearsal suffered a little, but then in court the testimony went quite smoothly.

MR: It did.

TS: And the judge used a couple of your points in his decision against the state of Arkansas.

MR: Not just a couple of my points. If you look at the judge's decision in *But Is It Science?*, his five or six criteria for what counts as science are taken precisely from my testimony. And you know, I'm not showing off—but that's what he did. And in fact, this is what got people like Larry Laudan[2] hot under the collar.

TS: There were some other well-known expert witnesses, too. Francisco Ayala, Stephen Jay Gould. In your book, you write a nice passage about them. You say, "To hear Ayala talking lovingly of his fruit flies and Gould of his fossils was to realize so vividly that it is those who deny evolution who are anti-God, not those who affirm it." What exactly are you saying here?

MR: I'm saying that if in fact you're Christian then you believe you were made in the image of God. And that means—and this is traditional Christian theology—that you have intelligence and self-awareness and moral ability. So what I would say then, that not to use one's intelligence, or to deny it or not to follow it, is at

---

[1] American Philosophical Association, which meets three times a year.

[2] Laudan is a philosopher of science who retired early (saying he was sick of the postmodernism that was taking over the university system) and now lives in a small Mexican town with his wife. Laudan was a critic of scientific realism and of claims that a clear line can be drawn between science and nonscience.

one level a heretical denial of one's God-given nature. And so this is the point I made—that in being a scientist, far from being anti-Christian or anti-God, you are utilizing the very things that make one God-like, in the Christian perspective. Of course, on the other hand, Christians are always caught up in this business of faith versus reason. And they love to argue that the most childlike among us can achieve understanding of God, true faith. So faith is very important for Christians. Nevertheless, it's a very important part of Christianity that our intelligence is not just a contingent thing, but is in fact that which makes us in the image of God.

II. "ETHICS IS AN ILLUSION PUT INTO PLACE BY OUR GENES TO KEEP US SOCIAL."

TS: Okay, let's talk about Darwinism and morality. Because on this topic, it's not just religious fundamentalists who object to an evolutionary approach. A wide range of people are disturbed by the idea that there could be any connection between Darwinian theory and ethics. Should they be?

MR: Yes, I certainly think they should be. In the past, evolution—Darwinian selection—has been used to legitimize some dreadful political and moral (for want of a better word) views. Hitler is open about his social Darwinism in *Mein Kampf.* Others have done the same. However, being disturbed is not to say that one should not take seriously the possible connection, because people have done bad things in its name. I would not reject the teaching of the Sermon on the Mount because priests have put their hands on little boys' willies.

TS: Do you think the connection has had some positive effects as well?

MR: Yes. In fact, historically one can make the case that social Darwinism has been a force for good as much as for bad. Alfred Russel Wallace used his evolutionism (and he was a codiscoverer of the theory of natural selection) to argue for socialism and feminism. People today also argue for things I find attractive. Sarah Hrdy argues that females are at least as successful as males and as dominant in their way, even though they use strategies that do not involve brute force. Ed Wilson argues for biodiversity in the name of evolution—he thinks if we destroy the rain forests, then we destroy humankind, and this is a bad thing. Of course what I would argue is that the connection between Darwinism and ethics is not what the traditional social Darwinian argues. He or she argues that evolution is progressive, that humans came out on top and therefore are a good thing, hence we should promote evolution to keep humans up there and to prevent decline. I think that is a straight violation of the is/ought dichotomy.[3]

TS: In your books you refer to this as a violation of Hume's Law. Can you explain exactly what Hume's Law is?

MR: I take Hume's Law to be the claim that you cannot go from statements of fact—"Duke University is the school attended by Eddy Nahmias"—to statements of value—"Duke University is an excellent school." Some say Hume was simply pointing to the fact that people do go from fact to obligation and was himself endorsing this move—but I think this is a misreading of Hume and certainly goes against his own philosophy.

TS: So then it seems that Ed Wilson, much as we support his cause, is guilty of violating Hume's Law, too. He's getting a normative conclusion—we *should* promote biodiversity—from facts about the way the world is. I know you two are friends—how does he respond to that charge?

---

[3] Ruse is referring to one of the most talked-about problems in ethics—the move from *is* to *ought*. The eighteenth-century Scottish philosopher David Hume was the first to point out that moralists tended to derive statements about what we *ought* to do from statements about the way the world *is*. But according to Hume, no one had ever provided the justification for such a move. Hume's work is extremely influential for many of the authors in this book because of his focus on the importance of emotions in moral decision-making.

MR: Ed does violate Hume's Law, and no matter what I say he cannot see that there is anything wrong in doing this. It comes from his commitment to the progressive nature of evolution. No doubt he would normally say that one should not go from *is* to *ought*—for example, from "I like that student" to "It is okay to have sex with her, even though I am married." But in the case of *evolution* he allows it. If you say to him, "But *ought* statements are not like *is* statements," he replies that in science, when we have reduction, we do this all the time: going from one kind of statement to another kind of statement. We start talking about little balls buzzing in a container and end up talking about temperature and pressure. No less a jump than going from *is* to *ought*.

TS: But you agree with Hume that the jump can't be made. Still, you want to say that there is some relationship between ethics and Darwinism, right?

MR: My position is that the ethical sense can be explained by Darwinian evolution—the ethical sense is an adaptation to keep us social. More than this, I argue that sometimes (and this is one of those times), when you give an account of the way something occurs and is as it is, this is also to give an explanation of its status. I think that once you see that ethics is simply an adaptation, you see that it has no justification. It just is. So in metaethics[4] I am a nonrealist. I think ethics is an illusion put into place by our genes to keep us social.

TS: An illusion—so then are you saying that the only true connection is that Darwinism can account for why we (falsely) believe that ethics is real?

MR: No, I distinguish normative ethics from metaethics. In nor-

---

[4] Metaethics is the business of trying to justify our ordinary ethical beliefs or systems. Normative ethics involves making judgments about how to behave (e.g., "It is wrong to put your hand on little boys' willies."). Metaethics examines the status of these judgments. Are they objectively true or false? Are they relative to specific cultures or species? These are metaethical questions.

mative ethics I think evolution can go a long way to explain our feelings of obligation: be just, be fair, treat others like yourself. We humans are social animals and we need these sentiments to get on. I like John Rawls's[5] thinking on this. On about page 500 of his *Theory of Justice*, Rawls says he thinks the social contract was put in place by evolution rather than by a group of old men many years ago. Then, in metaethics, I think we see that morality is an adaptation merely and hence has no justification. Having said this, I agree with the philosopher J.L. Mackie[6] (who influenced me a lot) that we feel the need to "objectify" ethics. If we did not think ethics was objective, it would collapse under cheating.

III. DOES MORALITY *NEED* TO BE OBJECTIVE?[7]

TS: What do you mean by that? The moral system *needs* us to think that ethics is objective?

MR: If we knew that it was all just subjective, and we felt that, then of course we'd start to cheat. If I thought there was no real reason not to sleep with someone else's wife and that it was just a belief system put in place to keep me from doing it, then I think the system would start to break down. And if I didn't share these beliefs, I'd say to hell with it, I'm going to do it. So I think at some level, morality has to have some sort of, what should I say, some sort of force. Put it this way: I shouldn't cheat, not because I can't get away with it, or maybe I *can* get away with it, but because it is fundamentally wrong.

TS: But what about chimpanzees and other species that engage in

---

[5] The Harvard philosopher, probably the most influential moral philosopher of the twentieth century. Rawls passed away in late 2002.

[6] The British philosopher, most famous for his book *Ethics: Inventing Right and Wrong*.

[7] In Chapter 8, Stephen Stich provides an in-depth discussion about whether we believe ethics to be objective and whether we need to believe that in order for ethics to function. Stich does not agree with Ruse on either of these questions.

altruistic, and some would even say moral, behavior?[8] They probably don't have any notions of objectivity and yet they still do it.

MR: I don't know that they don't. I would say that as soon as one starts to have some sort of awareness, then I would be prepared to say that there is some sense of objective morality—obviously much less than ours. When I come in and my dog looks guilty and I find it's because he peed on the carpet... I mean, sure, part of it is that he's afraid I'll beat the hell out of him, but by and large I don't beat the hell out of my dog any more than I do my kids. So I'd be prepared to say that the dog knows he's done wrong. Now, on the other hand, my ferrets—you know, they'll shit anywhere. I mean, I like ferrets, I love ferrets, but I don't think they have any awareness of right and wrong when it comes to these things. Whereas I really think that dogs and cats do, particularly dogs.

TS: I would definitely say dogs more than cats. Cats don't ever seem to think they're in the wrong.

MR: Right. And you know, I've talked to ethologists about this. Dogs are very social animals. And morality is a social phenomenon. And so in certain respects, dogs might be closer to humans even than, say, gorillas. And certainly orangutans. Orangutans are not particularly social beings at all. And so even though we're much closer phylogenetically to orangutans than we are to dogs, dogs have gone the route of sociality in a way that we have. So you might well find that something like a moral sense appears in dogs more than orangutans. I mean, that all sounds terribly anthropomorphic but it's not entirely stupid. Dogs work in groups, and that is what has made them the successful species that they are. They hunt together, share food. I mean, I'm not a dogologist. But I think it would be interesting to note, do you find cheating? Are certain dogs excluded at some level because they don't play the game?

---

[8] In Chapter 3, Frans de Waal discusses his views on primate and nonhuman morality as well.

I wouldn't be surprised if something like that happens. And you know, particularly at the chimpanzee level, there seems to be an awful lot of sophistication on who can be trusted and who can't be trusted, and who's cheating and so forth.

TS: And you would regard that as a belief in objectivity?

MR: Yes, I would. I don't feel the need to insist that they have a full awareness of objectivity, but it certainly seems to me that my dog shows a level of guilt and it's not just a matter of fear.

TS: It's true—I've never hit my dog in my life, but if she's ever done anything wrong, she looks guilty.

MR: Right, and you know exactly what she's done. But believe me, with ferrets, *guilt* is not a word in their vocabulary. We're like dogs, social animals, and so we have morality and this part of the phenomenology of morality—how it appears to us, that it is not subjective, that we think it *is* objective.

TS: But you've said that you think that at bottom there is no objective morality.

MR: The fact that you have a theory about something doesn't follow that you can do it. I mean, you can lie on the couch for years and the therapist can point out that your mother doesn't really hate you, but then you go out into the light of day and know that your mother hates you. What I'm saying is that human nature can't be turned over because of what a couple of philosophers are doing. I mean, David Hume makes this point. If you do philosophy, it all leads to skepticism. You can't prove a damn thing. But does it matter? No! We go on. I take Hume very seriously on this point. Our psychology prevents our philosophy from getting us down. We go on. We play a game of backgammon, we have a meal. And then when we come back to think about philosophy it seems cold and strange. So I think ethics is essentially subjective but it appears to us as objective, and this appearance, too, is an adaptation. It is not just that I dislike rape. I think it is *really and truly* wrong. Rawls of course denies that ethics is subjective, and as a Kantian thinks the answer is that the social contract is a condition of rational people living and working together. But I am inclined to think that rational people might have another social system different from ours. So, in a way, I am a Humean seeing morality as a matter of psychology.

TS: So it's not morality itself, but this feeling of *objectivity* in morality that is the illusion—right? But doesn't that mean that as clearheaded Darwinians, we have to say that there are no objective moral facts? And therefore that it is not an objective fact that rape is wrong?

MR: Within the system, of course, rape is objectively wrong—just like three strikes and you're out in baseball. But I'm a nonrealist, so ultimately there is no objective right and wrong for me. Having said that, I *am* part of the system and cannot escape. The truth does not necessarily make you free.

TS: The truth here being that there is no real right and wrong.

MR: Yes, but knowing that it is all subjective doesn't necessarily mean that I can become a Nietzschean superman and ignore it. I take very seriously Raskolnikov in *Crime and Punishment*. Dostoyevsky points out that even if we have these beliefs that there is no right and wrong, we can't necessarily act on them. And, you know, I see no real reason to get out of the system, either. If I rape, I am going to feel badly, apart from the consequences if I am caught. And the reciprocation—I don't want my wife and daughters raped. But even rape is relative in a sense to our biology. If women went into heat, would rape be a crime/sin? I wrote about this once in the context of extraterrestrials—is rape wrong on Andromeda?

TS: I'm not sure what you mean by "within the system it is objectively wrong." Do you mean that because we have laws and norms against rape, then rape is wrong? Or do you mean that for our species, given our biology, rape is objectively wrong? If it's the latter, aren't you violating Hume's Law, too?

MR: I would say that within the baseball system, it is objectively true that three strikes means you're out. It is true, but I would not say it's objectively true that George Steinbrenner should keep faith with Joe Torre. This latter is a Michael Ruse judgment call. There is no ultimate, God-given objective truth about baseball. It is an invention. There is no ultimate truth about morality. It is an invention—an invention of the genes rather than of humans, and we cannot change games at will, as one might change from baseball if one went to England and played cricket. Within the system, the human moral system, it is objectively true that rape is wrong. That follows from the principles of morality and from human nature. If human females went into heat, it would not necessarily be objectively wrong to rape—in fact, I doubt we would have the concept of rape at all. So, within the system, I could justify it. But I deny that human morality at the highest level—love your neighbor as yourself, etc.—is justifiable. That is why I am not deriving *is* from *ought*, in the illicit sense of justification. I am deriving it in the sense of explaining *why we have* moral sentiments, but that is a different matter. As an analyst I can explain why you hate your father, but that doesn't mean your hatred is justified.

TS: So then by analogy, Darwinian theory can explain why we have moral sentiments and beliefs, right? So let's get into the details. Why was it adaptive to have this moral sense? Why did our genes invent morality?

MR: I am an individual selectionist all the way. Natural selection has given us selfish/self-centered thoughts. It had to. If I meet a pretty girl and at once say to Bob Brandon,[9] "You go first," I am going to lose in the struggle for existence. But at the same time we are social animals. It's a good thing to be, we can work together.

---

[9] The philosopher of biology at Duke University.

But being social demands special adaptations, like being able to fight off disease and to communicate. We need adaptations to get on, and this I think is where morality comes in—or the moral sense—and other things like human females not going into heat.

IV. "YOU DON'T MAKE PROGRESS BY SITTING ON YOUR BUM FARTING ON ABOUT SPANDRELS."

TS: I wanted to ask this before—what is it about human females not going into heat that leads to us be moral?

MR: Human females not going into heat does not make us moral or immoral—but it is an important fact of our sociality and it is an important fact when we are making moral judgments (which are always matters of fact *plus* moral principles). I am simply saying that if women did go into heat, then even if we had the same moral principles—treat others fairly, etc.—it would simply not make sense to condemn someone for fucking the female if he got the chance. Having to take a shit is a physical adaptation, and it makes silly the moral claim that you ought never shit—although it does not affect the claim that it is wrong to go to your supervisor's home for supper and end the evening by crapping on his Persian rug.

TS: That's what I meant—why would it not make sense to condemn someone for raping a human female, if human females went into heat?

MR: Look, in my view, as a naturalist, I think epistemology and ethics are dependent on the best modern science. Look at Descartes and Locke and Hume and Kant. The point is that if women went into heat, then biology really would take over and we would lose our freedom. Have you ever been in a situation where you were sexually frustrated and didn't particularly want to jerk off but ended by doing so? Were you really a free agent? Or what if you are really hungry and there is a plate of french fries in front of you? Does one blame the alcoholic for drinking? I used to smoke and I would not say that I was free. The point is that *ought* implies a choice, and if women went into heat then there would be no choice. I wouldn't have a hell of a lot of choice even though they also wouldn't. So it's not that we are always moral—we certainly aren't—but we have the urge to be moral as one of the package of human adaptations.

TS: Okay, I can see why selection has given us selfish thoughts. A trait that leads you to give up the girl to Brandon every time is not going to get passed on to the next generation. Because you need a woman to pass on traits of any kind. At least for now, with the cloning ban. But adaptations that lead us to be moral seem trickier—especially those that on the surface would seem to decrease chances for survival and reproduction. Take for example the sense of guilt that we might feel when cheating on a spouse. Why would selection encourage a trait like that?

MR: I would be inclined to see guilt as part of the package of emotions that enforce morality. But I would never say that morality stops actions that are bad. Sometimes the guilt does stop adultery, but I suspect more often it is the fear of being caught.

TS: So then is the gist of this that morality has developed as a way of curbing some of our most antisocial or destructive tendencies? And that we have enough natural autonomy so that, sometimes at least, our moral sense wins out?

MR: That is right. We are a balance, or, if you like, a conflict, between selfishness and altruism. This is something that Saint Paul said a long time ago—but not everything that Saint Paul said is wrong. That is, whether the autonomy comes in. I think we are causally determined, but rather like sophisticated rockets that have the ability to redefine their targets in midflight as the new information comes in.

TS: This idea that ethics depends on the best modern science is still fairly unpopular among philosophers, isn't it? I was just at a weekend colloquium on "intrinsic value" and all the talk was about rights, human dignity, and rational agents—concepts that don't have much to do with science. Do you agree with your friend Ed Wilson's remark that the time has come for ethics to be removed from the hands of philosophers, and biologicized?

MR: Ed Wilson is given to too much rhetoric, but essentially I agree. Although there is a lot more interest in evolution and ethics than there was twenty years ago, and respectable people like Brian Skyrms and Elliott Sober have written on the topic.

TS: Both of these authors have developed naturalistic and Darwinian explanations for the evolution of altruism, or of the social contract. And both rely (in Skyrms's case, heavily) on game theory to support their claims. But game theory makes a lot of assumptions, some say unjustified assumptions, about inheritance mechanisms. How do you respond to the charge raised by Stephen Jay Gould and others that theories like theirs, and yours, are really "just-so" stories? That there is too little attention paid to the mechanisms through which complex behaviors, and something like a moral sense, could be passed along?

MR: I am sick of the criticism of "just-so" stories. Look at the volume on commitment just edited by Randy Nesse. There are lots of references to psychologists and others who are working on these issues empirically. Of *course* the game theory people make assumptions. That's how you do science. Get an idea, build a model, check it out, revise and redraw, etc. You don't make progress by sitting on your bum farting on about spandrels.[10] And you can quote me on that.

---

[10] Ruse is referring to a famous paper by Stephen Jay Gould and the Harvard biologist Richard Lewontin called "The Spandrels of San Marcos and the Panglossian Paradigm: A Critique of the Adaptationist Program." The authors criticize what they believe to be the overly simplistic approach of many Darwinian theorists.

TS: Done. Another objection I hear often is that if evolution can entirely explain morality, then moral nihilism is a consequence. Life has no meaning. We should all become like raving Dostoyevsky characters, or kill ourselves, or at least train ourselves out of any altruistic tendencies we might have and take advantage of everyone else. Now I can't see any reason why we should train ourselves out of anything, even if moral nihilism is true. Actually, the whole idea seems to violate Hume's Law. But it's undeniable that many people find the Darwinian worldview almost unbearably bleak. What would you say to some of these people?

MR: I think ultimately there is nothing—moral nihilism, if you wish. But I think Dostoyevsky was spot-on in *Crime and Punishment* to see that even if we see the full story, it does not mean that we can act on it, given our natures. Raskolnikov confesses of his own will, remember. But generally why should we try to go against our nature? It only makes us miserable. The only time I think it might make sense to try to step out of the moral game is if we saw that it was leading to worse things down the road. Again, Hume as always had the best response—backgammon and a good meal with your friends. Philosophy leads to skepticism, psychology lifts you out of it.

TS: So you wouldn't worry like some do about the cat being let out of the bag—about society at large coming to believe that morality was nonobjective?

MR: I certainly don't worry. I am far, far more concerned about the irrationality of the average American politician, especially Bush—stuff right out of fundamentalist religion about millennia and dispensations and raptures and that sort of thing.

TS: And to those who say something like, "If I thought that all there was at bottom were genes trying to replicate themselves, I'd kill myself," we can say, "No, you won't. You may think you would kill yourself, but you won't. Because you're a human being, and human beings like to have fun, play games, and drink with friends."

MR: Yes, but there's more than just that. I would also say that having Christian beliefs produces a fair number of heavy-duty psychological stresses and strains. I mean, I'm not quite sure that… Christ, the little fuckers, have they—no, I'm sorry, I thought they'd pissed on the carpet.

TS: Was that the dog or the ferret?

MR: The ferret. But they didn't. I mean, frankly, I find it a great relief to no longer believe in God. I don't know why it is but my God was always a bit of a Presbyterian. After creating heaven and hell and then humans, he spends the rest of creation, you know, hating them and making life miserable for them. I find it a great relief not to have that kind of God hovering over me.

TS: Is this a new development?

MR: To a certain extent. My father, who went from one religion to another, finally found peace of mind by arriving at a kind of Voltaire situation. You know, the best we can do is dig our garden, so let's get on with it. And so to a certain extent I find that very consoling.

TS: Overall, then, do you find the Darwinian view of the world to be an optimistic one?

MR: I don't find Darwinism optimistic or pessimistic—that is getting close to reading values out of a scientific theory—but I can live with it okay, and I find it exciting that we have the theory and can explore its full implications, scientific and philosophical, which for me are more or less continuous. ✶

5

JOSEPH HENRICH

RELATIVE JUSTICE

For much of the last century, the dominant economic model of human behavior was known as *Homo economicus*—a model which predicts that human beings will always act according to their (perceived) rational self-interest. Over the last twenty years, however, researchers in the flourishing field of behavioral economics have challenged this picture of human nature. Through the use of simple but ingenious experiments, these researchers have shown some of the ways that human beings systematically depart from self-interested behavior. The most famous of these experiments is known as the ultimatum game, and it works like this: subjects are randomly assigned into two roles, proposer or responder. Proposers are given twenty dollars and told that they can offer their responder anything between one dollar and the whole amount. Responders have two choices: they can accept and walk away with whatever amount the proposer has offered, or they can reject the offer, in which case neither the proposer nor the responder will receive any money at all. That's the whole game.

Now imagine that you're a subject in one of these experiments, and you're the responder. Your proposer is anonymous, but let's call him Doug. If Doug is a member of the species *Homo economicus*, his only concern will be to walk away with as much money as he can. He'll therefore be tempted to offer only one dollar and keep the remaining nineteen. Doug's only worry is that you'll reject the offer, in which case he will walk away empty-handed. But then Doug would think about it from your perspective. If you're also a member of *Homo economicus*, you'll accept any offer no matter how low it is. Why? Because one dollar is better than nothing, and nothing is what you'll get if you reject. So Doug can safely make the lowest possible offer of one dollar. And according to the model, you'll accept it.

But consider: how would you really behave in this situation? The choice to make Doug a proposer and you a responder was completely arbitrary. You don't deserve any less money than Doug, do you? The fair thing to do is to split the pot, right? And then he comes up with this insulting offer, one dollar, 5 percent of the total amount. Is that fair? Are you going to let him get away with that?

If you're like most readers, the answer is likely no. You'll gladly sacrifice the dollar to punish his greed. Nor is it likely that you'd have received such a low offer in the first place. In the experiments conducted in America in the past twenty years, the most common offer proposers make is a full 50 percent of the pot. And when low or unfair offers do come, responders tend to reject them, even in high-stakes games when the amount is still substantial. *Homo economicus* may not care about things like fairness, justice, and not getting screwed over. But it seems that human beings do—even at a cost to our own interests.

So where does Joseph Henrich come into this picture? As a graduate student in anthropology, Henrich was especially attuned to one drawback of these studies: the results were coming from a narrow range of subjects. Since the researchers were economists and psychologists working in universities, their participant pools were comprised almost exclusively of college students, mostly American.[1] Henrich had the brilliant idea of expanding the range of subjects not just demographically, but also culturally. He took the ultimatum game and other experiments to southeastern Peru and ran them with the Machiguenga, a family-centered forager-horticultural society scattered throughout the Peruvian Amazon. This kind of study was unprecedented in his field. Anthropologists are trained to do ethnography, to observe people in their natural environments and to describe what they see—no controlled experiments allowed. Henrich went ahead with the study anyway, and he came back with unexpected results. While the Machiguenga people did not behave in line with the *Homo economicus* model, they didn't behave like Americans either. For one thing, they didn't reject low offers in the ultimatum game. Further studies indicated that Americans and the Machiguenga have strikingly different ideas about fairness and justice, and Henrich's methods allowed him to measure these differences in quantifiable terms.

The study sparked a great deal of interest and led to a large MacArthur Foundation grant. The grant funded a large-scale project to conduct similar experiments in fifteen small-scale societies in field sites all across the globe. These studies revealed cross-cultural differences in attitudes about morality and justice in ways that no other analysis has been able to uncover. More generally, by incorporating methodologies from fields as diverse as anthropology, psychology, evolutionary biology, and experimental economics, Henrich and his colleagues paved the way for a revolution in the social sciences, a way of moving past the deep divisions among of the disciplines.

Joe Henrich was trained in anthropology at UCLA. He was an associate professor at Emory University before becoming the Canada Research Chair in Culture, Cognition & Evolution at the Uni-

---

[1] This is changing, but slowly. One study was coauthored by the economist Steve Burks, one of my old colleagues at the University of Minnesota, Morris, in 2005. He conducted ultimatum games with adult workers at a publishing company in Kansas City. Steve and his colleagues found that with nonstudent adults, the results tilted even more toward fair offers and fifty-fifty splits. Joe and Natalie Henrich have found this pattern repeatedly among nonstudents.

versity of British Columbia in 2006. He is the author, most recently, of *Why Humans Cooperate* (2007). I flew out to Vancouver to interview him this past summer, and returned home wondering why anyone would choose not to live in that city.

June 2008

I. *FEAR FACTOR* FOR ANTHROPOLOGISTS

TAMLER SOMMERS: You spent a lot of time—well over a year—with the Machiguenga, right? Did you bring back any good stories—especially ones that show some of the different ways in which they view the world?

JOSEPH HENRICH: One thing that really came across, and it happened to be going on while we there, is this. Missionaries contacted the Machiguenga in the middle of the last century. The missionaries wanted Bible translators, so they tried to get a democratic situation going. And so now each Machiguenga community has an official elected chief. They're in charge of getting development going in the village. The village is really just a cluster of independent families gathered around a school. And then in the rainy season, when school is out of session, everyone disappears to the forest. So there's one elected guy whose job it is to make sure the lawn gets cut and community buildings get built. And we watched day after day as this poor guy tried to get other people to help build the school. He'd blow his horn, no one would come. He'd go around door-to-door, maybe he'd get one or two people to help for a little while, but then they'd leave and go off to lunch. In the end, the teachers had to force the students to build their own school. And this is contrasted with these villages in Fiji I've been working in the last five years. They have chiefdoms, villages of about the same size, are similarly subsistence-based, on manioc and fish. But there, when the chief asks for help, everyone shows up, the whole situation runs like clockwork. The community buildings get built. Because they have norms about cooperation.

TS: And the Machiguenga just don't.

JH: They're ruggedly independent, to say the least.

TS: Right—in the book you say they would make the cowboy in the American Western look like a pathetic conformist.

JH: Yes.

TS: Any interesting anthropologist fish-out-water experiences?

JH: Well, the one I always think of happened when I first got off the plane. I think of it as my first real test as anthropologist. A woman came and saw us and brought out these bowls of *masato*. Traditionally, the Machiguenga would take manioc[2] and chew it up and then spit it into a pot and cook it. And the spit causes it to ferment, turning it into an alcoholic beverage.

TS: Is this the *chicha*?

JH: In other places it's called *chicha*, the Machiguenga call it *masato*. Really it's just chewed up manioc. I knew I'd have to be drinking essentially someone else's saliva. And when they gave it to me, it really smelled like vomit. I was able to sort of hold my breath and get it down.

TS: Sounds like a reality show. It's interesting; spit-based beverages came up in my interview with Steve Stich.[3] He used chicha as an analogy for moral claims, disgustingness claims. He thinks chicha is disgusting, but not that it's objectively true that it's disgusting. The Peruvians aren't wrong when they say that it's tasty. We project the disgustingness onto the world—the disgustingness seems like it's in

---

[2] A root vegetable and staple of the Machiguenga diet.

[3] See Chapter 8, p. 171.

the chicha, but really the disgust comes from within us. And the same goes for terms like *unfair* or *wrong*.

JH: Yeah, and it reminds me of another Machiguenga example of mine. Evolutionary psychologists often talk about food tastes being the product of evolution. And we might have some food tastes that are a product of evolution, but which foods we eat are much more culturally transmitted. I was hiking with the Machiguenga one time, and we decided to stop for a snack. They rolled over a log and picked up these long, slimy-looking larvae and started eating them. They like them because they're full of fat. I like fat too, but I didn't want to eat the larvae. That taste wasn't culturally transmitted to me.

TS: So the taste for fat in general is universal, but…

JH: Not the larvae.

II. PLAYING GAMES WITH THE MACHIGUENGA

TS: What gave you the idea to do the Machiguenga experiment?

JH: I was in graduate school in anthropology at the time. And we were working on a game theory model on the evolution of human cooperation. And repeated interaction models aren't much help in solving the toughest problem: what's called "n-person cooperation," a large number of people working together to contribute to some kind of public good.

TS: Because the opportunities to free-ride, to get benefits without paying the costs, are so numerous?

JH: Right. That's why it's a puzzle. But if you introduce punishment into the model, and have punishers who also cooperate, things work a lot better. So we were thinking that in the evolution of human cooperation, punishment is probably important. Rob Boyd, who was my advisor, had been going to interdisciplinary meetings, where he learned about the ultimatum game and behavioral economics. The rejections in the ultimatum game kind of felt like the sort of punishment we thought would be important. So then the idea to take it to the Machiguenga was this: the Machiguenga people live in small independent families scattered throughout the forest. There are no higher-level institutions, not much cooperation. If *they* punish, then we've really got something universal about human nature.

TS: You'd say "even the Machiguenga people" exhibit this kind of behavior.

JH: Right. They would be the toughest test case.

TS: But it turned out that the results were surprising, right?

JH: I wouldn't say that I was *positive* what they were going to do—but when I think about playing the ultimatum game, *I* would reject low offers. So I think I projected my intuitions on to them. I thought they'd reject low offers—they'd be like university students. And the paper I would write when I came back would be confirming the universal human disposition to punish at a cost, in the ultimatum game. But that's not what happened.

TS: I heard that you came back after a few months and told your advisor "I fucked up!" because the data were so out of line with what you were expecting.

JH: Well, I had to modify the protocol of the experiment so that we could run it in that environment, and there was a chance that I'd modified the protocol in some weird way, and that was the cause of the results. And there was also the concern that not only had I gotten the wrong answer but that people would *think* that I had somehow screwed it up. It's a natural assumption—I was an anthropology graduate student doing behavioral economics; it didn't seem like too much of a leap. So the first step in convincing myself was that I used the same protocol with graduate students at UCLA, and in their game the mean offer was 48 percent. So I was able to deal with some of those concerns.

TS: So what exactly were the results with the Machiguenga?

JH: Instead of a mean offer in the high 40s [45–50 percent of the pot]—which you see in America—they had a mean offer of 26 percent. And the modal offer, the most common offer, was 15 percent. And despite all those low offers, no one rejected.

TS: No one rejected?

JH: Well, there was one rejection, of a 25 percent offer, out of the whole sample. And always in my mind I have an asterisk next to that example, because we were looking for subjects to play, and found a Machiguenga woman who had been living in Cuzco [a large city in Peru] and hadn't lived in the village for many years. And she was the one person who rejected.

TS: What's your explanation for the differences in their behavior? Did you do interviews with them?

JH: Yeah, and none of them had the sense that somehow they were being screwed over, or that the first player had an obligation to make a high offer. It seemed quite sensible that they would get a low offer, and then faced with the choice of some money or no money, they took some money.

TS: There was no anger at the proposer because there was no real expectation that they would get a fifty-fifty offer in the first place?

JH: Right. They kind of hoped maybe to get a little bit more, but they didn't expect to get more. They viewed it more as bad luck to get the role of the responder.

TS: Like losing a coin flip to someone. It's unfortunate but you don't get mad at the person who won the toss.

JH: Exactly.

TS: Okay, so why do you think they have these attitudes?

JH: Well, I can now answer this question after a long time. I couldn't have answered it back when I first did the research. I now think that what we're measuring when we do this with university students and people in industrial societies are culturally evolved norms that have evolved over a long period of the evolution of human societies. And these are norms that allow us to interact in large-scale societies where we have lots of transactions with people we're not related to and won't see again. We don't know where they live, we don't know the names of their children. So we have all these norms that tell us that the right thing to do is split the pot fifty-fifty and we get mad when people violate that norm. The Machiguenga don't have that norm. And so to them, there's no expectation or rules about money in anonymous situations, and so they just do the self-interested thing, which is not to reject.

TS: You conducted these studies anonymously, right? No one would know who made fair or unfair offers. Do you think the results would have been different if the offers weren't anonymous?

JH: The next year we went—my now-wife (then girlfriend) Natalie and I—we did what are called "public-goods games." In these games, there are four players, and you contribute an amount of your personal allotment to a common pot and then the pot is doubled and divided equally among the group. The fully self-interested thing to do is to give zero. Actually, the way we did it, it's called a common-pool resources game. There are eighty dollars in a common pot, and each player can withdraw between zero and twenty dollars. And then whatever you leave in is doubled and then divided equally among the group. What a self-interested person does is withdraw all the money he can and then free-ride, and he still gets his share of what everyone left in the pot.

TS: Because the pot will only be doubled and then divided by four. So you're better off taking out what you can...

JH: Right. So if everyone is self-interested, all the money's gone and nothing doubles. We did this with the Machiguenga and then we also did it with students back in UCLA. The Machiguenga almost always withdraw the whole amount. They leave very little in the pot and very little gets doubled. And university students leave about half in. So there's a big difference there. Then we did two versions of this game among the Machiguenga. One where it was anonymous and one where you had to announce publicly what you were doing. And there was no difference.

TS: Really? Wow.

JH: People have trouble with this because they believe that our way of viewing reputation is the way everyone thinks about reputation. But among the Machiguenga they don't have these kinds of obligations to other families. They have obligations to their extended kin units and that's pretty much it.

TS: I take it there's a big change with university students when the game is not anonymous.

JH: Yes.

TS: So these surprising results led to a wide-ranging research program that examined behavior in fifteen small-scale societies, funded by the MacArthur Foundation. How did these studies work?

JH: Everyone did the ultimatum game. Some people did dictator games,[4] and some did public-goods games.

TS: There were two rounds, two generations of this project, correct?

JH: Yeah, so in the second generation, we took all the criticisms we got from the first and tried to address them methodologically. Because that's where we were weakest. There was some uncontrolled methodological variation between the sites. We fixed that up, and did a three-game package. We did a dictator game in every site, an ultimatum game, and a third-party punishment game. We kind of learned how to do it from the first project.

TS: So what's the take-home message from the results of that project?

JH: The take-home message is that there's a lot of variation in behavior. The Machiguenga and groups like the Tsimane in Bolivia, who have a similar lifestyle, hug the bottom end of the distribution, and they don't reject low offers. And then Westerners, especially Americans, are at the high end. We'll punish you if you screw us, and we'll be pro-social (altruistic). Even in the dictator game in America, where the responder has to take the offer no matter what, the most common offer is 50 percent of the pot. The mean is 48 percent. This is incidentally one of the main differences between students and nonstudent adults, the dictator game. Students are much more self-interested.

TS: So depending on your social and cultural environment, your behavior and your ideas about fairness are going to vary.

JH: Our hypothesis is that it has to do with the evolution of societal complexity, in particular—complex markets. One of our measures is the degree of market incorporation the society has. What

---

[4] These are games where the proposer can offer any amount and the responder has to accept. They have no option to turn the money down and send the proposer home with nothing. So the experiment is focused only on the proposer's behavior.

we think is that you have to have these norms about interacting with strangers in monetary contexts in order to engage with markets. Otherwise, your ability to engage in markets is limited to people you know. So complex large societies that are heavily engaged in markets have these strong fairness norms. And you need the norms to engage the markets. It's a two-way street. So you can live in this society and learn the norms. And the better people learn them, the more the market can be engaged. So this measure predicts the difference in offers.

TS: But there was variation among people who did have similar levels of market incorporation, right?

JH: Yes. Our measures of market integration capture about 50–60 percent of the between-group differences in offers. So there's a lot of unexplained variation. But that's still pretty good, given the crudeness of our measures.

III. "WE'VE FOUND *HOMO ECONOMICUS*! HE'S A CHIMP."

JH: You know, we've also done—I don't know if you've seen this work—we've done this with chimps too.

TS: You've done ultimatum games with chimps?

JH: Mike Tomasello and Keith Jensen did the ultimatum game with chimps. And we've done what's called a pro-sociality test, myself and Joan Silk and Dan Povinelli. In our task, chimps have two choices. Choice *a,* they get a food reward and another unrelated chimp gets the same reward. Choice *b,* they get the food reward and the other chimp gets nothing. So if you're purely self-interested, you're indifferent between the two because you get the same reward either way. If you care about others at all, you'll always pick *a,* to deliver the food to the other chimp. And if you're competitive, you'll always pick *a.* And it turns out that chimps are completely indifferent. They don't care.

TS: Huh. That wasn't my impression from *Every Which Way But Loose.*

JH: So I tell my economist friends that we've finally found *Homo economicus.* He's a chimp!

TS: But with the ultimatum game, you can measure rejection rates with chimps?

JH: Yes, that was the Tomasello experiment, and they never reject.

TS: But now, what about the experiment Frans de Waal and Sarah Brosnan did where the capuchin monkey throws away the cucumber if he sees the other monkey getting a grape?[5] He's mad that the other capuchin got something better; he thinks it's not fair.

JH: Yeah, I wrote a commentary on that for *Nature,* and Sarah Brosnan was a postdoc of mine, so I'm intimately involved with this. The problem with that experiment is that what the capuchins did is the opposite of what humans do. There's another version of the ultimatum game called the impunity game. And it's the same thing, except now if the responder rejects the offer, nothing will happen to the proposer. They keep their money. And when you do that with humans, they never reject. Because the whole point of rejecting is that they want to hurt the proposer, but now the responder can't do that. Now, when you go to the capuchin experiment, the capuchin throws away the cucumber because he wants the grape. But the other capuchin still gets to eat the grape. And we know humans wouldn't do that because this maps onto the impunity game.

TS: So the whole idea of de Waal and Brosnan's experiment was to show that capuchins have a rudimentary standard of fairness resembling ours. And your point is that *humans* don't even have that

---

[5] In the experiment, when two capuchin monkeys were given cucumbers, they both ate them. But when one capuchin got a grape (which they like much better) instead of a cucumber, the other capuchin refused to eat the cucumber and at times angrily threw it back in the face of the experimenter. Perhaps the capuchin was angered by the injustice.

kind of standard.

JH: Yes. Humans would be grumpy but they'd eat the cucumber. So if it's a standard of fairness, it's one humans don't have.

TS: And of course, if your work is right, humans have different standards of fairness anyhow.

JH: Yes.

IV. RELATIVE JUSTICE?

TS: Let's talk about the philosophical implications of all of this. Do you think your research undermines the idea that certain behavior is universally or objectively fair or just?

JH: Well, yes. I take an evolutionary approach. And from that perspective—I don't know much about philosophy—it's not even clear what an objective notion of fairness would mean.

TS: Just the idea that there's a certain standard of what's *really* fair or unfair, right and wrong. And if people like the Machiguenga violate those standards, they're making a moral mistake. Maybe it's not their fault, but it's a mistake nevertheless—just like being mistaken about the shape of the earth or something. Perhaps they aren't capable of understanding what's really fair and what isn't.

JH: Right. Well, if our theories are right, then beliefs about what you should do in the ultimatum game—and fairness norms in general—are just a product of a particular trajectory of cultural evolution, where you're building large societies in which strangers have to interact. And the other thing is: if you contribute to the group, say, the village or some larger part of society, you're contributing something that you could have been doing for your family. You're doing less for your family, more for everyone else. So one of the things about the evolution of complex societies is that there had to be a shift away from focusing only on your family and your kind, to focusing on these larger groups. So people say they value their families, but actually people in our society value their families a lot less than, say, the Machiguenga—who are entirely devoted to their families and don't allocate labor to society.

TS: So they might be appalled at how little we focus on the welfare of our brothers, sisters, and parents. They would consider *that* immoral. And your view is that there is no one correct answer to who has objectively right norms.
JH: Right.

TS: That's something many philosophers don't want to accept.

JH: So how do philosophers do this? I don't understand where "objectively correct" would come from. Because if I was going to evaluate the Machiguenga as wrong, I would need criteria. Keep in mind, I know nothing about philosophy...

TS: Well, there's the Kantian notion of the categorical imperative, that acts have to be universalizable.[6] Maybe the Machiguenga wouldn't be able to will that their acts became a universal moral law of nature. Or there's the utilitarian standard—some might argue that their behavior wouldn't result in greater overall happiness. Of course, the tough part is justifying that these principles—utilitarian or Kantian—are indeed objective standards of behavior. I talk about this a lot in my interviews with Steve Stich and with Josh Greene and Liane Young. It seems like the only way to show that these are the universally correct standards is to show that they capture our considered intuitions—our core beliefs, upon reflection. And if your work is on target, it seems like these core intu-

---

[6] The Kantian view, roughly, is that only actions whose maxims could be universalized are morally right or permissible. Breaking a promise is therefore forbidden, according to Kant, because if everyone acted on the maxim "Break promises when convenient," the institution of promise-making would collapse. The whole point of promises would be lost.

itions will be different.

JH: Definitely. The deep-seated intuitions are different across cultures.

TS: This reminds me of something [philosopher] Shaun Nichols told me—an interesting story you related to him about your research in Fiji. One of the native helpers where you were staying beat up his—was it his wife, girlfriend...?

JH: Yes, his girlfriend, but the mother of his child.

TS: And one of your assistants was talking with the girlfriend and her friends in the tent. And there was no sense that what happened was wrong. Is that accurate?

JH: Yeah, this was really awkward—one of those cultural-relativist moments where I really didn't know what to do. He was working for the project and sleeping in one of my project houses. And one of my graduate students was there. (I had a different sleeping house.) And suddenly she shows up at my door and tells me that Moavu, the guy, is beating up Nakuru, his wife or girlfriend. I knew the norm is that Fijian men can beat their wives; it's perfectly within their province to beat both their kids and their wife. So I made my presence known, and she ended up running by us. He saw us and ended up calming down a little. So I said something like: "Look, this is disgusting to us, so I don't know what I should do; I know that Fijians think differently about this." He decided to stop. But it was a problem, because he was my employee. So of course he stopped.

TS: But not out of any kind of shame.

JH: No.

TS: More like, I'm violating the etiquette of my boss, putting the fork on the wrong side...

JH: Right, right.

TS: It's an interesting test case for ethical relativism, tougher than these issues about fairness in ultimatum games. Obviously, they have different views about how to treat women. But how comfortable are you with the idea that there is no right or wrong answer about whether you should beat your wife whenever you feel like it? That it just depends on what culture you're in?

JH: My view is that it's wrong to beat your wife, but that there's no objective standard. It's just wrong for me to do it.

TS: So you're willing to say that it's not wrong for Moavu to do it?

JH: Right. Of course, it still disgusts me when he does it. But what I didn't do was go around the village and start preaching to everyone to change to my rules.

TS: That's interesting. Philosophers will go to great lengths to avoid accepting that implication.

JH: That you can't go around telling people what to do?

TS: Not that you can't go around *telling* people what to do exactly. But that it's not *actually wrong* for someone to beat his wife or girlfriend.

JH: The reason why you end up in the spot I'm in is this: once you get an idea about how these norms come about, this is a cultural norm that has a particular cultural evolutionary trajectory. So unless you think our society is on a special cultural trajectory, which I guess would be your out, but...

TS: You mean that we're on the right trajectory, and they've veered off onto the wrong one?

JH: Or they're stuck in some previous point.

TS: But your point still holds: from what standpoint could we justify the claim that our trajectory is the right one?

JH: Right. But just to finish the story—I wasn't present in the meeting of the girls afterward, but Tanya, my grad student, was. This woman Nakuru was beat up, really hurt, really sad. And so the women all sat around and they were comforting her. And several of them told stories about times they had been beat up. And I was asking Tanya who was mentioned—you know, I knew all the women and I knew all their men. And certain men I figured, there was no *way* that guy would do something like this. And sure enough: their wives had stories about the time these mild-mannered guys beat them up. I was shocked.

TS: And there was no indignation on the part of the women?

JH: Yeah. And the thing that made Tanya mad, I guess, was that Nakuru kept saying: "I should have listened to him. I shouldn't have been so social, talking to those guys."

TS: She was blaming herself...

JH: Right.

TS: Maybe this was an even more difficult test case for Tanya. Was she more tempted to preach about this being wrong?

JH: Yes, it was really hard for her. I told her what I thought, and I think she kept quiet... mostly.

V. TEAR DOWN THE WALLS!

TS: You have a new book out called *Why Humans Cooperate*, co-authored with your wife Natalie. It focuses on work your wife did with the Chaldeans, an Iraqi immigrant community in metropolitan Detroit.

JH: Yes, it started out as her dissertation, and we decided to transform that into a book incorporating a lot of theory and modeling that comes from evolutionary biology and economics. One reason why it's interesting to wrap the theory part around the anthropological research is that anthropologists typically write about small-scale societies. But here's a case where we find some of the same patterns in middle-class America.

TS: What patterns specifically?

JH: Well, we still find that kinship is important and reciprocity is important. But it manifests itself in different norms. So in a sense, there's this underlying evolved psychology, but it gives rise to interesting cultural variation.

TS: What is the variation as compared with other Americans?

JH: They have an ethnic identity, which is tied to their religion and language. They have strong ties to family and community, and so they have these small grocery stores, which are highly successful. But they avoid hiring non-Chaldeans, average Americans. And they have quite different norms about giving to charity. It's a big reputational hit if you don't give to Iraqi charities. They don't seem to care about other charities.

TS: Is it like with the Machiguenga, where if you give to a non-Chaldean charity that money could be going to help Chaldeans?

JH: Right, so it's actually bad to give to non-Chaldean charities. And they support political candidates who are Chaldean, which goes along with their sense of identity.

TS: A couple things about the book: one is methodological.

Your book brings together research from many fields within the sciences—mathematical modeling from evolutionary theory, behavioral experiments in economics, and thick ethnography.[7] This hasn't been done before, has it?

JH: As far as I know, it's not been done. Certainly not the particular combination of things we have. The problem is in the way social science works with the training. If you're trained in anthropology, you're trained how to do thick ethnography. You know zero about how to do experiments. But if you're trained in psychology—I'm in a psychology department right now—you learn how to do laboratory experiments with undergraduate kids, but you learn nothing about how to observe life and make systematic recordings about how people interact in real life. And in neither of those places do you learn much about evolutionary biology and how to make formal models of social interaction. So our effort is to pull all three together and show how each can tell part of the story and work synergistically.

TS: Is this the wave of the future of how to approach the puzzle of human cooperation? Should it be?

JH: Yeah, I think so. Human cooperation and a lot of other puzzles. We need to break down the walls between the social sciences. Everyone should learn multiple methods. And they should focus on problems and draw from whatever techniques and methods they need to solve that particular problem. There should be no reason why a psychologist shouldn't go out and live in a community and do some ethnography that's accompanied by a bunch of experiments.

TS: In philosophy, there's a movement afoot to try to tear down

---

[7] Natalie Henrich spent a year and a half living in Detroit, studying the Chaldean culture —talking to them about their norms, values, behavior. This kind of long-term detailed observation is known as thick ethnography.

traditional walls between philosophy and the sciences. Philosophers who do this run into a lot of over-the-top hostility and resistance.[8] Do you get that in the social sciences? People trying to defend their turf?

JH: Let's see. There's definitely a core in anthropology who are completely hostile to this approach. They think experiments are unethical.

TS: Why?

JH: That's a good question. I guess they think experiments force people to do things they wouldn't normally do. So you're sort of paying them to be unethical. It's a little bit unformed, but I know about this in particular here at UBC because when I was recruited here, the dean called me up and wanted to hire me. So he figured, this guy's an anthropologist, we'll put him in the anthropology department. I did my talk there and the department pretty much rioted. They said this guy does experiments, this guy does math, and he thinks evolution affects human behavior.

TS: Really? The dominant view in anthropology is still that evolution has no effect on how humans behave.

JH: Yeah. It's fine for talking about stones and bones, but any kind of interesting social behavior—no. This is cultural anthropology. There's also biological anthropology—but there was only one biological anthropologist here at UBC and now there's zero.

TS: And your view is that evolution does play a large role in influencing human behavior, but that it interacts with culture, too, and there's this feedback between the two.

---

[8] See the interview with Stephen Stich in Chapter 8 for more about turf wars in philosophy.

JH: Right, so you need evolution and you need gene-culture co-evolution, which means that part of our genetic evolution has been shaped by culture. And then there's just plain "We're a cultural species, we're heavily reliant on learning from other people." That's just cultural evolution. All of these things play a role in explaining human behavior, and the relative importance depends on the particular problem one is examining.

VI. "WHY DO YOU LIKE MASHED POTATOES?"

TS: Something I found fascinating that came out of my interview with Steve Stich [see p. 199 of this book] is this: according to Steve, there are many cultures in which people don't feel much of an urge to morally justify their behavior. You talk about this in your book as well.

JH: Yeah, people don't have these elaborate explanations for why they have their beliefs, or why they should do things the way they do them. Sometimes it's even awkward interpersonally, because it's like you asked a stupid question. It's similar to, well, if you like mashed potatoes and I ask, "Well, why do you like mashed potatoes?"

TS: So that's the right analogy. It's like asking them to justify tastes?

JH: That's what it feels like when you're asking them. They have this look: "How am I supposed to know? That's just how it is."

TS: There's a hypothesis that Steve came up with based on this. I'll quote him directly: "The tradition of trying to justify normative claims in a deep and foundational way, the tradition of trying to provide something like philosophical or argumentative justifications for moral judgments—this is an *extremely* culturally local phenomenon. It's something that exists only in Western cultures and cultures that have been influenced by Western cultures. For much of human history, providing that kind of justification has played no part in normative psychology." Would you go along with that?

JH: I do think that we have a culture of elaborate post-hoc construction. The only thing I'd say is that I'm not sure how much of just a Western phenomenon this is. I have a friend who studies ancient China and it sounds like they have a tradition of this as well—of trying to figure out why we have the beliefs we do. So it could be complex societies that sit around and think about these things. So that's a possible exception, but I'd need to learn more about ancient China before saying anything definite.

TS: Do you think there's some kind of cultural environment that lends itself to this kind of justification?

JH: Well, maybe—this is off the top of my head—it could be that it arises when you have to formalize law. You have judges. So you get into this situation, a legal rhetoric. You've got to explain it, you've got to reapply it, it could be then that you might develop this tradition.

TS: And the cultures that you've found that don't have this tradition of justification—there's no legal system at all?

JH: Well, in places like Machiguenga and Fiji, there's a national legal system which exists somewhere out there, but it doesn't affect day-to-day life. And it's not relevant to things we're asking them about. So I'm trying to think of another analogy. It might be like asking, "Why do you love your children?" The only sensible answer to me would be an evolutionary one.

TS: And that's sort of a different level of explanation.

JH: Right, it doesn't answer why *you* love your children. You just love them, that's all there is to it.

VII. DEMOCRACY FOR EVERYONE?
NOT SO FAST.

TS: What do you do when you go on these expeditions? I don't really know the details of how these anthropological studies are conducted. How you interact with the people, what you tell them. For example, your research in Fiji. How does all that work?

JH: When we first arrive, we give a formal presentation to the chief and to the community, and tell them what we're up to. And then we've been living there—well, I have people there now almost full time. We run interviews, I hire various Fijians from universities there. We do work on a whole bunch of different topics, we're working on lots of different things at the same time. Interviews, experiments, and then just observing daily life.

TS: That's standard procedure? That's what you did with the Machiguenga?

JH: I developed this over the years. The typical anthropological study wouldn't involve many research assistants. So I've developed a kind of corporate version of this. It's on a much larger scale. I use experiments; other anthropologists don't use experiments. We're like psychologists except we do all of this ethnography. We sample people randomly to see what they're doing throughout the day. We study social networks.

TS: Are there conflicts that come up? Resentments, people wondering what you're doing there?

JH: Generally, the community is very supportive of it. It provides a lot of benefits to the community. We do some of the games and people get money, and they love that. We have to buy food when we're there, and that brings benefits. We have had some problems with outsiders, who start up a little trouble when I get some money from the project. So it's not without conflict.

TS: But nothing from inside the community.

JH: No, in fact people really like that we're interested. I've been working on the language, and they love that an outsider can come in and talk to them in their local dialect.

TS: What do you think the social and practical implications of your research are?

JH: One practical implication of all this is that things like formal institutions, legal systems, laws, formal government, they have to be well-fitted to the informal local norms. And so what you can't do is take a formal system from one place and just plop it on top of another place, and expect it to work. Because there's no fit. That seems to have all kinds of implications for economic development, for all kinds of things.

TS: Maybe a certain war we're engaged in? Trying to bring our values, democracy, to a region where it might not fit—is that something you'd think is unwise?

JH: Sure, that definitely comes to mind. Of course, the Iraq situation is just the latest installment of this same notion that happened a lot throughout Africa. Instituting a British parliamentary system or something like that. And it's really hard to get these things to work because it doesn't fit with the local system of values. The idea of doing democracy in a Fijian village, for example, is actually insulting to people there because they have a hierarchy that's based on the chief. And we've been studying why they think the chief has the right to make these decisions. They have an existing system which isn't a democracy, although it does give equal voice to everybody. But it is a decision-making system. If you tried to just stick a democracy in there, I can't imagine what would—things just wouldn't go well.

TS: The norms are too entrenched for that to work.

JH: Yeah. One way to do it would be to start with some area of social life that's not well developed, and try to stick it there. Because people don't have preexisting norms that are being violated. And then maybe gradually you could spread out from there, slowly replacing these other systems.

TS: But aren't their own norms working for them, given their cultural environment? Would it be fair to say that in some types of environment, democracy just isn't suitable?

JH: Yeah. The only way to make it work would be to change the way everyone thinks. And that takes a very long time.

TS: Has your research affected your day-to-day behavior in any way?

JH: Yes. I think having an awareness of the power of culture to shape our brains and our moral beliefs—well, rather than being arrogant about your views, you're more ready to accept that that's what the other guy believes...

TS: Jon Haidt said something along those lines, that he feels less indignant, even when it comes to political issues.[9]

JH: Yeah, Jon has great examples on this. Because something that hits home for a typical liberal academic would be Republicans, red-state types. I think a lot of my fellow academics think that they've got the right moral values and those people in... rural Missouri have the wrong ones. So once you have this perspective, you might still have your liberal beliefs—I know Jon and I share a bunch of those—but we're not as belittling as some of our colleagues. We don't think people who disagree with us are evil idiots. We understand how you can have these basic differences in how you view the world.

---

[9] See Chapter 7, especially sections III and IV.

TS: It's interesting that Steve Stich disagreed with that. He said he feels just as strongly about his views, even though he agrees with you on all the empirical issues about the origins of these beliefs. I guess he thinks that some types of moral beliefs involve an attitude that other people should stop doing the practices you find immoral, no matter who they are.

JH: Right. Well, even so, I think with this perspective, the approach you would use to persuade someone to stop would be quite different. If you think they're evil idiots, or just need to be informed or something, that's different than saying they're perfectly well-informed and they just have a different interpretation of the facts that we share.

TS: A different interpretation?

JH: Suppose you and another person are viewing a painting. You think it's beautiful and the other person thinks it's ugly. What Jon and I are suggesting is that we've realized that you and the other person may be looking at the same painting through quite different lenses, each distorting the painting in different ways. Your lens distortions lead to a pleasing judgment. You can't remove the lens, or easily see through the other person's, but you can realize we're each using a different lens to judge the same painting. My view is that efforts at persuasion can be fine, by getting others to use your lens. The issue is really about realizing a certain degree of humility with regard to the certainty of our own moral tastes. ✶

6

JOSHUA GREENE
AND LIANE YOUNG

TROLLEY PROBLEMS

Here's the situation. A trolley is racing down the tracks, out of control, and will kill five unsuspecting workers unless you act. You're standing at a switch that can divert the trolley to a second track where there is only one unsuspecting worker. Should you flip the switch?

Most subjects in studies posing this dilemma say that you ought to flick the switch. The reasoning is simple: if you act, one person will die instead of five—a net gain of four lives. But watch what happens when the scenario is adjusted in one small but apparently significant way: the same trolley with the same dead conductor is barreling down the track, headed for the same five unsuspecting workers, but this time there is only one track, and you are on a footbridge, looking down at the situation. In front of you is an unsuspecting fat man. You know that if you push the fat man over the bridge, his girth will be enough to stop the train. He'll be killed, but the five workers will be saved. Should you push him over the bridge?

Now the results are completely different. The vast majority of subjects think that it would be morally wrong to push the man in order to stop the runaway trolley. What's puzzling is that in many ways the scenarios are identical. In both cases, your act causes one man to die—who wouldn't otherwise—instead of five others. There's that same net gain of four lives. The only difference is that in case one you're flicking a switch, and in case two you make physical contact with the doomed man. What accounts for the radical difference in our moral intuitions?

Philosophers working in the tradition of Immanuel Kant have one answer. In the footbridge scenario, you would be using the fat man as a "mere means" to save five people; you intend to kill him in order to achieve the desired end. Kant's categorical imperative prohibits you from using another rational human being against his will to achieve an end, no matter how worthy. Each human being (no matter how fat) has infinite worth—dignity—and must be treated as an end in himself. This is Kant's big disagreement with the utilitarians or consequentialists, who believe that acts are morally right insofar as they bring about the best outcome. In the trolley switch case, you're not using the single worker as a means to an end—at least not directly. The death is an unfortunate side effect of your act of flicking the switch. So, many neo-Kantian philosophers would say that we correctly perceive the moral wrongness of pushing the man over the bridge, and this accounts for the near-unanimous intuition that we shouldn't do it.

But there's another angle here, too, and this is where cognitive neuroscientists Joshua Greene and Liane Young come into the picture. Joshua Greene, a philosophy Ph.D. at Princeton before turning to psychology, had a hunch that the reactions to these cases had very little to do with a rational understanding of Kantian imperatives and much more to do with our evolved moral psychology. Greene suspected that certain emotions, which were once adaptive for human beings, motivate the different judgments in these cases and others like them.[1] So as a postdoc at Princeton, he presented these scenarios to subjects in a functional MRI machine (a machine that measures brain activity). The results confirmed his prediction: areas in the brain associated with emotions were activated in the footbridge-style up-close-and-personal cases, but not in the impersonal trolley-switch cases. The thought of pushing someone over a bridge triggers our emotions in a way that flicking a switch does not, even though the end results in terms of loss of life are identical.[2] Greene then developed a dual-process model to account for this. According to the model, our reasoning faculties motivate our utilitarian intuitions, the ones that tell us to perform the act that will produce the greatest happiness or least amount of suffering. And our emotions motivate our deontological judgments: we recoil at intentionally harming someone even if doing so reduces the amount of total suffering. The experiment, along with Greene's fluid writing style and dynamic presentations, launched his career and resulted in his appointment to the psychology department at Harvard.

Meanwhile, Liane Young, then a rising star in Harvard's Psychology graduate program—and now a postdoc in the Department of Brain and Cognitive Sciences at MIT—was developing her own ingenious career-launching experiment to determine the role of emotion in moral judgment. What's the best way to find out how emotion contributes to moral decision-making? Find subjects who don't have any emotions to contribute! (Well, it's a little more complicated than that, as you'll see…) I began my interview by asking Young to describe this study, which had recently appeared in the journal *Nature*.

March 2008

---

[1] Greene discusses another, more practical example, one originally developed by the philosopher Peter Unger. If you drove by a bleeding hiker with a broken leg because you didn't want the blood staining your car's leather upholstery, you'd be a moral monster. But spending $400 on leather upholstery rather than donating that money to a charity that could undoubtedly save someone overseas from losing a limb seems perfectly acceptable. What's the morally relevant difference between these two cases?

[2] The experiment was celebrated for the insight it offered and also for the new avenues of investigation that it opened. Although the practice is now relatively common, no one before Greene and his colleagues had thought to run brain scans on subjects as they made moral judgments.

I. TO KNOW BUT NOT TO FEEL

LIANE YOUNG: The basic idea was to investigate the role of emotion in moral judgment by looking at how patients with severe emotional defects make moral judgments. More specifically, we set out to test a new model of moral judgment that Josh put forth, on the basis of his first two fMRI studies—the dual-process model. Josh found neural evidence for the role of emotion in rejecting harm and the role of "reason" in going for the greater good. So we were able to test Josh's dual-process model by looking at a population of individuals with deficits in emotional processing due to brain damage.

TAMLER SOMMERS: What kind of patients exactly?

LY: When I say "population," I really mean six patients. These patients are quite rare; they have very specific lesions in a part of the brain responsible for emotional processing—but the brain is intact everywhere else, and thus so are their other cognitive functions.

TS: They can still do logic problems, math problems, they can reason about consequences.

LY: Right. The site of their brain damage happens to be in the front of the head, right behind the space in between the eyes, and is known as the ventromedial prefrontal cortex, or VMPFC. The VMPFC, when it's working properly, in healthy individuals, responds robustly to stimuli with social emotional content. Like pictures that instill fear in a majority of people—Sarah Palin as our vice president, for example, or more seriously, war scenes or pornography. Patients with damage to the VMPFC, though, don't produce normal emotional responses to such stimuli. So, for example, if you and I saw pictures of mutilated bodies, our hearts might start racing, our palms might start sweating, and so on. And if we saw a scan of our brains, we would see activity in the VMPFC. But when you give the same emotional stimuli to VMPFC patients, all the measurements—heart rate, skin conductance—appear flat.

TS: So how did examining these subjects test Josh's dual-process model?

LY: We sat participants in front of the computer, and they read and responded to scenarios one by one, the original scenarios constructed by Josh for his fMRI study. Their task was to judge whether they would perform a particular action if placed in the shoes of a character in the scenario. The moral scenarios were divided into two groups: impersonal and personal. Impersonal moral scenarios weren't particularly emotionally salient; the harms were impersonal in nature. Personal moral scenarios were emotionally salient; the harms were, as Josh describes them, "up close and personal." So, for example, a classic impersonal scenario is the trolley problem with the guy at the switch. And the personal scenario is the footbridge case. The difference boils down to flipping a switch versus pushing a man. So what we found was that patients with VMPFC damage produced the same patterns of responses on the impersonal scenarios as people without the damage.

TS: Just as likely to say that they would flip the switch as normal patients....

LY: Yes, but on the personal scenarios, VMPFC patients were more likely to endorse harming one to save many. More likely to say they'd push the man over the bridge, for example. They were more willing to go with the numbers, to go with the consequences. In other words, VMPFC patients showed themselves to be moral utilitarians, maximizing welfare, in line with Josh's dual-process model.

TS: Interesting. Because they didn't have the emotional responses to the direct infliction of harm.

LY: Yes, emotional processes allow us to respond to harms, especially those that are up close and personal, like pushing the man off the bridge. These emotions often cause us to reject these harms.

Cognitive processes support abstract reasoning, including utilitarian reasoning—figuring out how to bring about the best outcome Moral judgment in VMPFC patients is dominated by the cognitive processes, and therefore comes out utilitarian. So Josh's model provided just the right level of detail for systematically testing emotion in specific moral judgments.

TS: Let's turn to that. Josh, how did you come up with your model, and the idea for testing it?

JOSHUA GREENE: In high school, I did a philosophically oriented debate, and I remember thinking that utilitarianism made a lot of sense to me. Someone in a debate round presented me with the transplant problem. So I was arguing that we should always do the greatest good for the greatest number, and someone said: "Oh yeah? Well what about if you could kill one healthy person and give all of their organs to five healthy people who need them? Would that be okay?" And I was stumped. I said, "No, I guess it wouldn't." And I was struck by that. Because I thought that I had a pretty good—well, you know, me and John Stuart Mill—that we had a pretty good theory, and then this person really stumped me.

Then in 1995, I read [Antonio] Damasio's book *Descartes' Error.* I remember the moment. I was in Israel at my sister's bat mitzvah, I was sitting in the hotel room alone reading, and I stood up in my bed, and said "This is it!" That is, I read the description of Phineas Gage—the man who survived a steel rod cutting through his skull and giving him brain damage in regions of the brain associated with emotion. Damasio describes his condition as "to know but not to feel." And I thought: that's what's going on in the footbridge case. There's this feeling that "this is wrong," and that *feeling* is different from the *thought* "I know it makes sense to kill one person to save five." And I immediately thought: I bet if you tested patients with emotional deficits like Gage, they would be more utilitarian. And actually, the first study I had in mind was just like the study Liane described. And then when I was at Princeton I heard there was this new guy in town who set up a brain-imaging center and was interested in talking to philosophers. So I went to see him. He's a very no-nonsense guy. He just sat back and said, "Okay, shoot." I told him about the trolley problem, and Phineas Gage. And he said, "Oh, yeah," and he was on board right away. And that was how I ended up in the Cohen lab.

TS: So your experiment along with Liane's shows how our emotional responses lead us to make anti-utilitarian judgments in these up-close-and-personal cases. How do you think this research bears on the status of those intuitions? In other words, how do these studies bear on the *justification* of utilitarian and Kantian intuitions?

JG: My primary goal was to explain the intuitions, to understand why we say yes sometimes and no other times—

TS: Without justifying them?

JG: I certainly wasn't interested in justifying the intuitions as they are. If my theory was right, you could interpret the results as debunking the Kantian intuitions.

TS: Can you explain what you mean by *debunk*, exactly?

JG: A debunking explanation is one that explains why we have a belief in a way that makes it unlikely that the belief is true. For example, you might believe that you are having a conversation with a lampshade, and then you might explain away (i.e., debunk) that belief by appealing to the fact that you recently ingested LSD.

TS: And you thought our Kantian emotional responses might be affecting our moral judgments the same way LSD affects our judgments about whether lampshades can talk?

JG: In a very abstract sense, yes. But this analogy has limitations, of course. An LSD trip is an unnatural experience for which our brains were not designed. Moral emotions, in contrast, are part of normal, adaptive brain function. Despite these differences, the idea is that both explanations—you were hallucinating and you were having an emotional response—can undermine judgments made under those circumstances, depending on your assumptions about whether LSD-induced hallucinations or emotional responses are likely to reflect an independent truth.

II. SELECTIVE DEBUNKING

TS: This leads to a key question for me about Josh's work, or at least the implications of his work. You say you're a debunker, and you focus on debunking the Kantian intuitions. In the end you want to support the moral theory of utilitarianism. You want to debunk all the intuitions but the utilitarian ones.

JG: Right...

TS: But I never figured out how that fits with your general moral skepticism—your view that no moral beliefs are true, including utilitarian beliefs. I would think that as a moral skeptic you would deny or debunk *all* moral intuitions, not just the intuitions that aren't consistent with your favorite theory.

JG: Well, right, I don't think utilitarianism is the right theory, the *true* theory. But I do have utilitarian values. That is: I think that happiness and suffering are things that matter. They matter to me. I also think everyone's happiness and suffering matters equally. That more suffering is worse than less suffering. That more happiness is better than less happiness. Those are values I can't let go of. And those postulates that lead to utilitarianism, I can't shake them. And I see no reason to shake them. By contrast, the kinds of intuitions that guide Kantian or deontological thinking, like "Well, if you intend to kill all those people, that's really bad; but if you intend something else, while at the same time *knowing* that those people will die as a side effect of your bombing the munitions factory, that's not so bad"—well, *that* I'm skeptical of!

TS: Skeptical in what sense, though?

JG: Look, the people are just as dead! And you know just as much that you're killing them. Why should it matter that you didn't specifically intend for them to die? Why should we care about that distinction? I have the immediate *feeling* that it matters. I have the feeling like other people do. But why does it make it okay to kill people just because it's not what you're going after? Who cares what's going on in your head! They're dead! So I've always been skeptical of those kinds of deontological distinctions that seem bogus. And that's my motivation for studying those stances. Trying to understand them in proximate causal terms (e.g., this is just an emotional response) and—I think this is crucial—in evolutionary terms. Explaining why for *nonmoral* reasons we might have these moral intuitions. And that's where the real debunking happens. And so, to answer your question—how can you be a moral skeptic and a utilitarian at the same time—I don't think utilitarianism is true. I think it's what you're left with after you've disavowed all the stuff that is arbitrary or contingent or not hard to let go of when you understand where it came from.

TS: Liane, you want to break in?

LY: Yes. So, it's also going to be emotional responses to harm and suffering that's leading you to those fundamental principles of utilitarianism, right?

JG: Yep. I have a grad student who's working on finding those emotions right now.

LY: So even though it's not the *same* emotions that are grounding utilitarian intuitions rather than Kantian intuitions, they're still emotions, right? Because I always thought that your debunking account of Kantianism was grounded by the fact that principles were rooted in emotional responses, and that emotion was an unreliable source for moral judgments, that they exert biases in illicit ways.

But utilitarian principles are also grounded in emotions, so...

TS: Right, it seems like you could run the same debunking argument on utilitarian principles.

JG: This is really an important and complicated issue. I think that Hume and Liane are right that all moral evaluation has to have some kind of affective or emotional basis. What I would want to focus on, then, are the different kinds of emotions that are involved and what they're sensitive to. In the trolley case that Fiery [Cushman] and Liane did, for example, it turns out that we have different emotional responses to killing someone when our own muscles are involved in moving the person, rather than just relying on gravity. [Subjects find it more wrong to stop the trolley by pushing someone over a bridge than by releasing them via a trapdoor.] And this is where the rubber meets the road. Are emotions sensitive to things that upon reflection we think ought not to matter?

TS: Then the key issue for you is how we regard the emotional responses upon reflection?

JG: Yes. Now, I think that no one would say—I'm sure some philosopher somewhere would, but no sane person would ever say that it's morally important in and of itself whether you touch the person to harm them or use a trapdoor to harm them. But our emotions are sensitive to that difference. And that leads to differences in judgment. By contrast, if I have a sense of sympathy for someone who suffers or a basic feeling of approval when someone becomes happier or has their situation improved, that's not something I'm inclined to disavow after I think about it. So I think what it really comes down to is not "emotions bad; cognition good." It's all emotional on some level. It's rather that some emotions are more rigid and inflexible and sensitive to things that we wouldn't ever think are morally important.

TS: So emotions that you would endorse upon reflection are good (but not true), and emotions that you would not endorse upon reflection are bad (but not false)?

JG: Right—with full information, including scientific information that we're only just beginning to gather. So in a sense, I have a coherentist moral epistemology.[3] I don't think that utilitarianism or any other moral theory comes out of the sky as a correct moral theory. I have certain values, intuitions, and beliefs about how the world is and how the human mind is, and as I reflect about the tensions within my own values and intuitions and try to understand them scientifically, I think that some of those values stand up pretty well to this kind of scrutiny, and others wither. And the more I've learned, the more I've become skeptical about Kantian intuitions, and confident that our utilitarian intuitions are perfectly respectable.

TS: Well, that leads to my next question. Let's say I also have another intuition that it's morally appropriate for me to value my daughter's happiness over the happiness of a total stranger's daughter. It's just as basic as your utilitarian beliefs, and one that I'm just as likely to endorse upon reflection. But this intuition goes against the utilitiarian principle that we should value everyone's happiness equally. Why should I junk my intuition in favor of the utilitarian one?

JG: There are two ways to respond to that. One is to say, look, some things are just nonnegotiable. Morally speaking, I don't think my child's welfare is morally more important than anyone else's. But I have no illusions about the fact that this is not a bias that I can overcome. And because other people have this bias, it would be disastrous to try to make people overcome it. So from a policy perspective, it would be ludicrous to try to get people to care equally about all children. And from a personal perspective, it would be ludicrous for me to try to talk myself out of that state. So maybe

---

[3] Roughly, this is a view that the right or most reasonable moral system is one that is the most consistent within itself and with other nonmoral beliefs.

ideally if I was rewriting the species, I'd write out the partial-to-your-children inclination, but I still don't think it's wrong to love my wife and child more than, you know, many other—

LY: —than you love me and Tamler.

JG: Well, you guys are great…

LY: But fundamentally you've got to accept that there's nothing morally wrong with being partial to your children. Right?

JG: I think we all have that belief. And then we learn about Darwin, about natural selection, and kin selection. And if you're me, you get to the point where you say: "Okay, so maybe that belief isn't ideally morally justified, but it's just a feature of our psychology."

TS: But as you said, there's also an evolutionary story for why we care about anyone at all—why we have an aversion to the suffering of other people, for why we have the utilitarian intuition. Why isn't that just a feature of our psychology? In other words, what I'm still struggling with is: you seem to think that Darwinism debunks my intuition that it's morally justified to value my daughter's happiness over the happiness of somebody else. But natural selection doesn't debunk your utilitarian intuition. It's selective debunking. Why is one principle more debunkable than the other?

JG: Well, that's an interesting question. There's a tension between the utilitarian intuition and the kin-selection, partiality-to-your-children principle. In the face of that tension, which does it make more sense, intellectually, to give up? That the most happiness is good? Or that it's good for me to care about my offspring, even if that doesn't produce the most happiness? I don't know if I can spell this out further. Maybe I can, but one seems more basic, more fundamental than the other. You can imagine a world in which everyone cares about each other equally—their own children as much as anyone else's. And everyone was wired that way. That's still a recognizably moral world. Whereas a world in which everyone is indifferent to the happiness of others doesn't strike me as a moral world at all. So maybe therein lies the asymmetry. I'm actually working this out for the first time and I think it's something I need to spell out.

LY: But that's still a value judgment about which world is better. And that's just an appeal to another intuition.

JG: I think it's an appeal to a conceptual notion of morality. You can imagine a world that everyone would term "moral" without one principle: partiality to kin. But you can't imagine a world that anyone would term moral where no one cared whether people suffered or were happy—it was all the same to them. And that's what makes the utilitarian intuition more fundamental. I'm actually really glad this came up, because it's where my [recent] article ends,[4] and I haven't yet tried to formulate this. But in any case, I want to reiterate that there's a difference between these kinds of arguments and what the Kantians do, which is to ignore the scientific explanation for their emotions and pretend that there's some deep reason, some philosophical justification for their intuitions when instead it's just this post-hoc cop-out.

TS: But isn't there a third option? To be fully aware of the science behind my intuition? To say, "Look, I know all about why I'm partial to my children, I know all about kin selection. And I don't care!" I stand by that intuition. If that means I have to diverge in some cases from another intuition I have, so be it. Who says there needs to be this one universal principle that guides all my actions anyway?

JG: You don't have to believe there's only one universal principle. But you do want to believe that your moral intuitions aren't arbitrary, right? The problem with the thoroughgoing pluralist view

---

[4] Greene is referring to an essay called "The Secret Joke of Kant's Soul," which attempts to expose the emotional basis behind our Kantian judgments.

you're defending is that you do take yourself to be acting for reasons. Morality presents itself as objective to us. And if you're admitting that you have this intuition, then you could have had another one, and, well, you're ending up having to accept that morality comes down to a set of whims.

LY: But morality is always going to come down to that in a sense, right? There is no independent way of justifying any principle or theory—whether it's utilitarian or Kantian.

JG: Right. Which is why I'm no longer a moral realist. So now I think the best we can do is try to get to your core bedrock values, the ones that it's inconceivable to give up. And starting with those, make everything as consistent as possible. Both internally consistent and consistent with what we know about how your mind works, how human nature works, and where it comes from.

TS: Okay, let me try to frame my question a different way. Back in the day, when I was denying free will and moral responsibility...

JG: Always a dangerous thing...

TS: Tell me about it. Inevitably, at some point, people would say: "What if someone harmed your daughter Eliza? You wouldn't think he was morally responsible for doing that?" Well, I had a couple of responses. First, psychologically I wouldn't be able to think that person didn't deserve blame or punishment. In fact, I'd want to give the guy as much punishment as possible with my bare hands. With something like that, your retributive emotions override any kind of theory you have in your head. But then I thought about something else, something that made me question even my theoretical skepticism about free will and moral responsibility.[5] Even if I *could* somehow use my theory to overcome or

---

[5] This thought has led to a slight shift in my views on responsibility since my interview with Galen Strawson (Chapter 1) in 2003.

undermine my retributive hatred of this person, I wouldn't want to. I actually think there'd be something *wrong* with me if I didn't have that irresistible inclination. In other words, it's *not* an ideal version of me that would abandon retributive feelings toward a person who hurt Eliza. And so that makes me think that there is something deeper about our attachment to our children. It's not just something that makes us think, Look, we have it, we can't get rid of it, so let's enjoy it. To me, having this attachment is about as deeply right as anything else we could possibly believe.

JG: So is it that you think it's deeply *right* to have that attitude, or that you think it's deeply *you*?

TS: I think something would be wrong with me if I could overcome it. I'll say it like that.

JG: Well, let me put it this way. I don't think it would be wrong of me to rewire my brain so that I became a more perfect utilitarian. Imagine if I could rewire my brain so that all I do is make money and give it away to poor people in an efficient way. Now, would I choose to do that? Well, I wouldn't choose to do that. But that's essentially because I'm partial to *myself*. And part of what it is to be *me* is to have these nonideal values. So it wouldn't be wrong to rewire myself into a kind of utilitarian saint. But I don't want to. And the reason why I don't want to is that I want to continue to *exist*. Another way to think about it is: Imagine if I could kill myself and bring to life someone who was morally better than myself, according to my criteria. I wouldn't want to do that, because I want to exist as someone recognizably *me*...

TS: So it's a personal-identity thing. That's interesting.

JG: Yes, it really becomes exactly that: a personal-identity issue. If I were to rewrite my desires, I might come out better according to my own standards, but *I* wouldn't come out.

III. META-METAETHICS

TS: So Liane, let me ask you—because I know something about Josh's metaethical views, but I don't know about yours—

JG: I don't either, actually. We've never really talked about it.

TS: How have your fMRI studies and your work with patients with emotional deficits affected your view of morality in general?

LY: Hmm. I don't know if I've come to a conclusion like Josh has about what my metaethical views are, based on the data of my experiments and others. I guess my views are still evolving.

TS: What are the candidates?

LY: One possibility is to take a closer look at my intuitions and ensure that I can at least come up with some kind of justification for those intuitions. That seems like a bare minimum, but it clearly isn't enough.

JG: Although it is a substantive test, right? You can't do that with some of those more deontological intuitions, like ones that involve body contact or no body contact.

LY: True, but nor do I want to, in some cases, and that's another interesting thing to think about. In what cases am I motivated to try to come up with a justification for my intuitions, and in what cases am I totally content to dismiss my intuitions? I think one of the reasons I give more weight to certain intuitions than Josh or Singer or other utilitarians is those "meta-intuitions" that tell me when I ought to put in the effort to justify an intuition, and when I should be content to dismiss it as a bias.[6] Or, on the flip side, when I believe that some principles are fundamental, and I should stop

---

[6] This is the key question in the debate between the three of us. How do we know when an intuition is a bias rather than a reflection of a reasonable moral belief?

looking for justifications. I can't seem to wrap my head around those meta-intuitions. That's not to say I'm going to stop trying, but it seems like there's a whole other layer of intuitions that I don't think we're studying, intuitions that guide our *inquiry* into the intuitions we are studying.

TS: So if I get this right, Josh has a meta-intuition that his intuitions should be as consistent as possible with each other, and they need to come from sources that he trusts. Your meta-intuition is that sometimes it's just okay to have either inconsistent intuitions or intuitions that can't be unified by one principle.

LY: Are you trying to say I'm less coherent than Josh?

TS: Well, maybe I am, but not in a pejorative sense—I have that feeling too, sometimes. Why couldn't you have a general framework that allows for a plurality of different conflicting principles?

LY: It's not exactly that—you say that in Josh's view, the sources of the intuitions matter, and all the intuitions should cohere together nicely, and for me I have intuitions about whether certain sources of moral judgment are legitimate or illicit sources.

TS: Okay—intuitions about what counts as a debunking explanation, and what counts as a plain old explanation.

LY: And it's those intuitions that I don't understand, and therefore think that maybe there's some role for those intuitions in my overall view of morality.

JG: Yeah, so I think Liane and I both want to have a coherent value system, but that maybe we have different starting points. I've been a skeptic my whole life. I'm relatively ready to abandon intuitive common sense beliefs in favor of what I think is better. Whereas other people are going to have a higher standard of evidence required before they jettison something that makes intuitive sense to them.

IV. TO PUSH OR NOT TO PUSH

TS: One question I always like to ask is how you apply your own theories to your everyday life and your research. I'll start with Josh. You accused John Rawls of constructing an entire theory of justice, an entire methodology, just to justify his intuition that utilitarianism was morally objectionable. Well, a much less sympathetic person than I am could say: Josh, look at your story. You started out as a utilitarian as a kid, as a high-school student, and now you've constructed, through your work and your research, a kind of justification of utilitarian principles. Boy, *that* worked out nicely. How *convenient*. How maybe post-hoc. Now, I'm not saying you're doing that, but I wonder: do you *worry* that you're doing the same thing that you're accusing Rawls of doing? After all, your own theory—Jon Haidt's theory, too[7]—would predict that you would be doing exactly that.

JG: I think it's a very good question. I've been asked something along those lines before, and I had to admit that the view came first, and the research came later. And I can't help being a little embarrassed by that history, but I think I can be vindicated. I think what's going on—not to sound obnoxious—but I think I'm a pretty insightful person, and I was intuitively skeptical of what one ought to be skeptical of. Certain nonutilitarian intuitions seemed fishy to me—and so I was able to further justify that skepticism. There was a time when I wasn't so confident, like when I got hit with the transplant problem, all the counterexamples to utilitarianism. And so I delved into those counterexamples. It could have happened that I would have found intuitive yet clear and sensible reasoning behind those intuitions, kind of like what Rawls would hope for—these subtle but normatively plausible principles behind them. If that were the case, then I might have said: "There's a wisdom here, à la Leon Kass." But instead what I found were heuristics, biases,

---

[7] See Chapter 7.

and emotions. Along with an evolutionary story that makes the reliability of those emotions questionable. And so I've had an up and down. But now I've arrived at a kind of steady state where I'm comfortable as a subjectivist utilitarian. But the ride to get here wasn't totally smooth.

TS: And you think you've avoided the temptation to cook the books in your own way.

JG: You never know for sure. I've only just gotten started, and it's true that so far I've devoted most of my resources to experiments that show that my theory is right.

TS: What about you, Liane? You haven't been doing this stuff for quite as long, but do you worry about the temptation to use theories—scientific theories—to justify your initial intuitions?

LY: Again, I feel like you always start out with these intuitions, what we value. Josh started out with utilitarian intuitions, I didn't. We had different starting points. Now I've evolved more toward Josh's view, but not all the way. You seem to start out with these priors and then throw out anything you can't come up with good reason to justify. And it seems like the language that we use for deontological intuitions is post-hoc rationalization. Mostly. But in the case of utilitarianism, we talk about sensible reasonable accounts rather than rationalization, but I'm not sure if the difference is that stark.

JG: But I don't see how there's any rationalization going on with utilitarianism! Everybody is a utilitarian to some extent. Everyone thinks that outcomes matter.

TS: All things being equal.

JG: Yes, all things being equal, everyone thinks it's better to have less suffering than more suffering. Everyone applies those principles.

It's just a question of whether you also have other principles in there to override them.

LY: First, just because everyone does it, that doesn't mean everyone isn't rationalizing. But second, I think there are other non-utilitarian principles that everyone shares and everyone thinks are fundamental. Everyone thinks intentions matter, or more broadly that what happens in the mind matters, and not just in a utilitarian way. So in the same way that people are utilitarian to some extent, people are all nonutilitiarian to some extent. They think people's beliefs and intentions matter independent of the usefulness of taking those things into account. To the same extent that they think that outcome matters.

TS: So then let me ask you, Josh. If you're on the footbridge behind the fat man—do you think you should push him?

JG: Personally, I wouldn't feel comfortable doing it. After all, I'm only human. But if someone else were to do it, and do it for the right reasons, knowing that it would work, I wouldn't condemn it.

TS: Liane?

LY: Well, I've certainly got the easier job here, because for this case at least my squeamishness about pushing people off bridges is supported by my intuition that it's morally wrong to do so. Maybe it's just the emotions talking, but I suspect that there really is more to the moral story than consequences. How the story plays out exactly over the next few decades will be interesting, but my bet is that it'll have something to do with intentions, maybe not in the trolley-problem sense, but generally what's going on in our heads when we act—doing not just the right thing but, like Josh said, for the right reasons. So I guess this is my long way of saying, no, I wouldn't push the man. I think there's more to morality than maximizing consequences. ✻

PART III

BAD WIZARD, GOOD MAN: DISPELLING THE ILLUSIONS OF MORALITY

L ike our sex lives, our moral lives offer plenty of opportunities for deception and self-deception. The interviews in this section address some of the illusions about ethical practice to which we're susceptible. For example:

I arrive at my moral judgments through reason.
One popular idea about moral decision-making is that we deliberate. We weigh both sides of the issue, and after sufficient reflection, we make the best ethical call we can (much like Randy Cohen in his popular *New York Times Magazine* column, "The Ethicist.") In Chapter 7, Jonathan Haidt argues that this model is mistaken for most people, most of the time. Our emotions fuel our judgments, and our reasoning is often post hoc—it comes after the fact to justify the conclusion we've already reached.

Educated people share my core values and intuitions.

Next, philosopher Stephen Stich argues that most ethical theories (as well as theories in other areas of philosophy) rest on a "problematic bet" that there isn't substantial variation in philosophically important intuitions. Evidence from anthropology and cultural psychology suggests that the bet is all but lost. Stich explores the implications of this variation and arrives at a complex and subtle position about how we should regard moral values that may have no universal or objective foundation.

As a member of the enlightened West, I have progressed beyond the primitive ideals of honor, status, and vengeance.

Baloney, says legal theorist William Ian Miller in our final chapter. Imagine if Mandy Patinkin's lines from *The Princess Bride* went: "Hello. My name is Inigo Montoya. You killed my father. Prepare to be rehabilitated." Would *The Princess Bride* still be the classic it is today? Do audiences root for Clint Eastwood to *forgive* Gene Hackman at the end of *Unforgiven*? Miller defends the nobility of cultures that emphasize the importance of honor and revenge, and argues that these values still pervade our lives whether we admit it or not.

7

JONATHAN HAIDT

COMFORTABLY DUMBFOUNDED

These are indignant times. Reading newspapers, talking to friends or coworkers, we often seem to live in a state of perpetual moral outrage. The targets of our indignation depend on the particular group, religion, and political party we are associated with. If the Terri Schiavo case does not convince you of this, take the issue of same-sex marriage. Conservatives are furious over the prospect of gays and lesbians marrying, and liberals are furious that conservatives are furious. But has anyone on either side subjected their views to serious scrutiny? What's the response, for example, when conservatives are asked exactly why gays and lesbians shouldn't be allowed to marry? "It threatens the institution of marriage." Okay. How? "Marriage is between a man and a woman." (Some liberals give this answer as well.) Right, but why? "It's unnatural." Isn't that true of marriage in general? "Well...

look... I mean... it's just wrong!"

If you're familiar with the work of Jonathan Haidt, it will come as no surprise that resentment, disgust, and outrage are rarely supported by fully developed arguments and deliberation. A psychologist at the University of Virginia, Haidt has devoted his career to the study of moral judgment and decision-making; his results are revealing and perhaps a bit unflattering. We tend to think of ourselves as having arrived at our moral judgments after painstaking rational deliberation, or at least some kind of deliberation, anyhow. According to Haidt's model—which he calls "the social intuitionist model"—the process is just the reverse. We judge and then we reason. What, then, is the point of reasoning, if the judgment has already been made? To convince other people (and also ourselves) that we're right.

To support his model, Haidt has devised a number of ingenious experiments. He presents scenarios designed to evoke strong moral responses ("It's wrong!"), but ones that are hard to justify rationally. (Examples include: having sex with a chicken carcass you're about to eat, wiping your toilet with a national flag, and, as we'll see, brother-sister incest.) Although the goals of these experiments vary, the results all point to the causal importance of emotions and intuitions in our moral life, and to different roles for reason from the ones we might expect or hope for. Haidt's model goes against some dominant trends in moral and social psychology, in particular the theories of well-known psychologists Jean Piaget and Lawrence Kohlberg, whose work appeared to support rationalist models of moral judgment (where reason plays the primary causal role in moral decision-making). But as Haidt himself notes, his own work can be placed within a grand tradition of psychology and philosophy—a return to an emphasis on the emotions which began in full force with the theories of the Scottish philosopher David Hume.

One last thing to say about Jon Haidt: he gives the best conference talk in the business. There are slides, great visuals, videos of fraternity guys trying to explain why sleeping with one's sister is wrong, images of a toddler perturbed about not getting the same number of stickers as the child beside her (or, in one hilarious case, a three-year-old who isn't perturbed at all), and plenty of sharp insights and jokes. The research Haidt presents has implications for philosophy, anthropology, psychology, and even the culture wars in America; not surprisingly, it provokes controversy and lively debate. I interviewed Haidt after a conference at Dartmouth College.[1]

May 2005

I. REASON IS THE PRESS
SECRETARY OF THE EMOTIONS

TAMLER SOMMERS: I want to start out talking about the phenomenon you call "moral dumbfounding." You do an experiment where you present five scenarios to a subject and get their reaction. One of these scenarios describes a brother and sister—Julie and Mark—vacationing in the south of France. They have some wine, one thing leads to another, and they decide they want to have sex. They use two different kinds of contraception and enjoy it, but they decide not to do it again. How do people react to this, and what conclusions do you draw from their reactions?

JONATHAN HAIDT: People almost always start out by saying it's wrong. Then they start to give reasons. The most common reasons involve genetic abnormalities or that it will somehow damage their relationship. But we say in the story that they use two forms of birth control, and we say in the story that they keep that night as a special secret and that it makes them even closer. So people seem to want to disregard certain facts about the story. When the experimenter points out these facts and says, "Oh, well, sure, if they were going to have kids, that would cause problems, but they're using

---

[1] Since this interview took place, Haidt's work has garnered quite a bit of attention in the popular press. His book *The Happiness Hypothesis* appeared in 2006, and lately it seems that a month can't go by without op-ed columnists from the *New York Times* and elsewhere referring to his research.

birth control. So would you say that it's okay?" And people never say, "Ooh, right, I forgot about the birth control. So then it *is* okay." Instead, they say, "Oh, yeah. Huh. Well, okay, let me think."

So what's really clear, and you can see it in the videotapes of the experiment, is: people give a reason. When that reason is stripped from them, they give another reason. When the new reason is stripped from them, they reach for *another* reason. And it's only when they reach deep into their pockets for another reason, and come up empty-handed, that they enter the state we call "moral dumbfounding." Because they fully expect to find reasons. They're *surprised* when they don't find reasons. And so in some of the videotapes you can see, they start laughing. But it's not an "it's so funny" laugh. It's more of a nervous-embarrassment, puzzled laugh. So it's a cognitive state where you "know" that something is morally wrong, but you can't find reasons to justify your belief. Instead of changing your mind about what's wrong, you just say: "I don't know, I can't explain it. I just know it's wrong." So the fact that this state *exists* indicates that people hold beliefs separate from, or with no need of support from, the justifications that they give. Or another way of saying it is that the *knowing* that something is wrong and the *explaining* why are completely separate processes.

TS: Are the subjects satisfied when they reach this state of moral dumbfounding? Or do they find something deeply problematic about it?

JH: For some people it's problematic. They're clearly puzzled, they're clearly reaching, and they seem a little bit flustered. But other people are in a state that Scott Murphy, the honors student who conducted the experiment, calls "comfortably dumbfounded." They say with full poise: "I don't know; I can't explain it; it's just wrong." Period. So we do know that there are big differences in people on a variable called "need for cognition." Some people need to think about things, need to understand things, need to reason about things. Many of these people go to graduate school in philosophy. But most people, if they don't have a reason for their moral judgments, they're not particularly bothered.

TS: So your conclusion is that while we might *think* that reason or reasons are playing a big causal role in how we arrive at moral judgments, it's actually our intuitions—fueled by our emotions—that are doing most of the work. You say in your paper that reason is the press secretary of the emotions, the ex post facto spin doctor.

JH: Yes, that's right.

TS: What do you mean by that, exactly?

JH: Reason is still a part of the process. It just doesn't play the role that we think it does. We use reason, for example, to persuade someone to share our beliefs. There are different questions: there's the psychological question of how you came by your beliefs. And then there's the practical question of how you're going to convince others to agree with you. Functionally, these two may have nothing to do with one another. If I believe that abortion is wrong, and I want to convince you that it's wrong, there's no reason I should recount to you my personal narrative of how I came to believe this. Rather, I should think up the best arguments I can come up with and give them to you. So I think the process is very much the same as what a press secretary does at a press conference. The press secretary might say that we need tax cuts because of the recession. Then, if a reporter points out to him that six months ago he said we needed tax cuts because of the surplus, can you imagine the press secretary saying: "Ohhhh, yeah, you're *right*. Gosh, I guess that *is* contradictory." And then can you imagine that contradiction changing the policy?

TS: I'm having a hard time doing that.

JH: Right. The president dispatches the press secretary, and the secretary's job is basically to lie—to just make up a story. Should I take that back? No, I won't take that back. The press secretary's job is to be a *lawyer*. To argue for a position. And he doesn't need to con-

sult with the president about what the real reasons were for instituting the policy. Those are irrelevant. He just needs to build the
best case he can.

TS: You brought this up in your talk at Dartmouth, and I like the
analogy. You said that when it comes to moral judgments, we think
we're scientists discovering the truth. But actually we're lawyers arguing for positions we arrived at by other means. So, setting aside
a few philosophy graduate students, do you think this is how our
moral life works?

JH: For most people, most of the time, yes. There's a question of
what you could call the ecological distribution of moral judgments. Now, by moral judgment I mean any time you have a sense
that someone has done something good or bad. Think of how
often you have that sense. If you live in a city and you drive, you
probably have that sense many times a day. When I read the newspaper, I think unprintable thoughts, thoughts of anger. So I think
moral judgment is ubiquitous. Not as ubiquitous as aesthetic judgments. As we walk around the world we see many beautiful and
ugly things. But we don't deliberate about them. We just see things
as beautiful or ugly. My claim is that moral judgment is very much
like aesthetic judgment. In fact, whenever I'm talking with philosophers who are trying to get me to clarify what I'm saying, if
I ever feel confused, I just return to aesthetic judgment, and that
saves me. I think whatever is true of aesthetic judgment is true of
moral judgment, except that in our moral lives we do need to justify, whereas we don't generally ask others for justifications of aesthetic judgments.

TS: So now where do these moral intuitions come from? I guess
I'm looking to see if you think they're a product of evolution.

JH: Yes, I do. We're born into this world with a lot of guidance as
to how to make our way. Our tongues come with various recep-
tors that make us respond well to fruit and meat. Our bodies are

designed to give us pleasure when we encounter fruit and meat. And to get displeasure from bitter sensations. So our bodies are designed to mesh with properties of the real world, the real *physical* world—to track nutrients and poisons.

Similarly, our minds come equipped to feel pleasure and displeasure at patterns in the social world. When we see someone cheat someone else, we feel displeasure, dislike. And this dislike is a signal to us to avoid that person, to avoid trusting that person or cooperating with him. When we see a heroic act, or an act of self-sacrifice, or charity, we feel an emotion that I call moral elevation. We feel a warm, very pleasurable feeling that includes elements of love. We're much more likely to help such people, to trust them, and to want relationships with them. So just as our tongues guide us to good foods and away from bad foods, our minds guide us to good people, away from bad people.

TS: And having these feelings was adaptive—they contributed to greater individual fitness—in the time we did most of our evolving?

JH: Yes. There are a couple of watersheds in human evolution. Most people are comfortable thinking about tool use and language use as watersheds. But the ability to play non-zero-sum games was another watershed. What set us apart from most or all of the other hominid species was our ultrasociality, our ability to be highly cooperative, even with strangers—people who aren't at all related to us. Something about our minds enabled us to play this game. Individuals who could play it well succeeded and left more offspring. Individuals who couldn't form cooperative alliances, on average, died sooner and left fewer children. And so we're the descendants of the successful cooperators.

II. DREW BARRYMORE: HOT OR NOT?

TS: I want to talk about the philosophical implications of your model for a moment. When I came across your work, I thought it provided a good deal of support for a position we can describe as moral skepticism. In particular, I thought the social intuitionist model makes plausible the claim that there is no such thing as objective moral truth, even though human beings *believe* that some of their moral judgments are objectively true.[2] But you don't draw skeptical conclusions from your findings, do you?

JH: For me it all hinges on the distinction made by David Wiggins between anthropocentric truths and nonanthropocentric truths. If anybody thinks that moral truths are going to be facts about the universe, that any rational creature on any planet would be bound by, then no such facts exist. I think that moral truths are like truths about beauty, truths about comedy. Some comedians really are funnier than others. Some people really are more beautiful than others. But these are true only because of the kinds of creatures we happen to be; the perceptual apparatus—apparati—that we happen to have. So moral facts emerge out of who we are in interaction with the people in our culture.

TS: So you would call those *truths*? Take someone like Drew Barrymore—some people find her fairly hot while other people don't see what the big deal is. You would say that there is some *truth* concerning what her aesthetic appeal really is?

JH: Well, apparently, if there's that much disagreement about her, she must be somewhere in the middle. There's much less disagreement about Catherine Zeta-Jones and George Clooney. So they are more attractive than Drew Barrymore.

---

2 For those who are philosophically inclined, my thinking is as follows: We have moral intuitions. These intuitions were not selected for their ability to "track moral truth," nor were they even selected for their contributions to human happiness. They were selected because they enabled individuals and their relatives to leave more offspring. At the same time, though, these intuitions lead us to believe that the truth of our moral judgments is self-evident. (Think of the Declaration of Independence.) So to me it seems that Haidt's model lends some support to what philosophers call an error theory of morality—a theory that attributes widespread error to human beings about the status of moral claims.

TS: So in other words, the way you determine the truth is by how much agreement there is?

JH: It's not that simple. But these are truths in which how people respond is the most important piece of evidence. You could never say that person X is really hot even though nobody thinks so. I think about it this way. One of my favorite quotes is from Max Weber: "Man is an animal suspended in webs of significance that he himself has spun." So I think that with morality, we build a castle in the air and then we live in it, but it is a real castle. It has no objective foundation, a foundation outside of our fantasy—but that's true about money, that's true about music, that's true about most of the things that we care about.

TS: So give me an example of some ethical truths in the limited sense that you're talking about.

JH: Let's see... you should value and repay those who are good to you. You should protect and care for those who you are superior to, in a dominant position to. You should not hurt people unless there's a very good reason to do so—where good reason means a moral reason, not just a reason advantageous to yourself.

TS: So let's take one of those: you should take care of those people who are in an inferior position to you—

JH: You have a position of authority over them... so you should take care of them.

TS: What makes that true?

JH: What makes that true... what makes that true... now I feel like I'm the subject of one of my own dumbfounding experiments.

TS: Well, that's what I'm wondering. Why isn't this one of those cases?

JH: Nothing *makes* it true—it's a truth that grows out of who we are... what makes that true... See, I guess that's the wrong question. This is—I know that philosophers are very into justifications but... nothing makes it true.

TS: Okay, but then how—

JH: Well, okay, let's see. Catherine Zeta-Jones is beautiful—what makes *that* true? Um, her... shape, I suppose.

TS: But don't people think that there's a difference between moral truths and aesthetic truths? If someone doesn't find Catherine Zeta-Jones beautiful, for whatever reason, you don't necessarily think that he's *wrong*, do you?

JH: I might, actually.

TS: Most would think that maybe he just has different tastes. Maybe he likes blondes, he likes men, he hates the Welsh, or whatever. But now take a moral judgment, like "It's wrong to torture people." If someone says, "No, it's not wrong at all... it's fun, actually, you should try it," you don't just think: To each his own. You think he's *wrong,* that he's made a mistake. And that's where you want justifications—you want to be able to convince people that they're wrong in a way that has nothing to do with their individual preferences on the matter.

JH: That's right. So we need justifications for our moral beliefs; we don't need them for our aesthetic beliefs. We can tolerate great diversity in our aesthetic beliefs, but we can't tolerate much diversity in our moral beliefs. We tend to split and dislike each other. I recently wrote a paper on moral diversity, addressing the fact that many people, especially in academic settings, think that diversity is a virtue in itself. Diversity is not a virtue. Diversity is a good only to the extent that it advances other virtues, like justice or inclusiveness of others who have previously been excluded. But people are wrong when they say that everything should be more diverse—even, say, rock bands. It's an error, an overgeneralization. I'm sorry—back to your question. And this relates to the distinction between moral pluralism and moral relativism. I subscribe to the former, not the latter.

TS: What's the difference?

JH: What I want to say is that there are at least four foundations of our moral sense, but there are many coherent moral systems that can be built on these four foundations. But not just *anything* can be built on these four foundations. So I believe that an evolutionary approach specifying the foundation of our moral sense can allow us to appreciate Hindu and Muslim cultures in which women are veiled and seem to us to lead restricted lives. These are not necessarily oppressive and immoral cultures. Given that most of the world believes that gender-role differences are good and right and proper, these cultures are unlikely to be wrong—by which I mean, they are unlikely to be incoherent or ungrammatical moralities. We in America, especially liberals, use only two of these four bases. Liberals use intuitions about suffering (aversion to) and intuitions about reciprocity, fairness, and equality.

But there are two other foundations—there are intuitions about hierarchy, respect, duty… that's one cluster. And intuitions about purity and pollution, which generate further intuitions about chastity and modesty. Most human cultures use all four of these bases to ground their moral worldviews. We in the West, in modern times especially, have to some extent discarded the last two. We have built our morality entirely on issues about harm (the first pillar), and rights and justice (the second). Our morality is coherent. We can critique people who do things that violate it within our group. We can't critique cultures that use all four moralities. But we *can* critique cultures whose practices are simple exploitation and brutality, such as apartheid South Africa or the American slave-owning South.

TS: Okay, but *why* is it that we can critique apartheid South Africa whereas we can't critique a culture that uses genital mutilation where chastity and fidelity of females is considered a high virtue? What makes us able to do one and not the other?

JH: You have to look at any cultural practice in terms of what goods it is aiming for. Veiling, or keeping women in the home, is usually aimed at goods of chastity and modesty. Not all human practices are aimed at moral goods. Sweatshops, child pornography, child slavery, the slavery of Africans in the American South—none of these is aimed at goods provided by any of the four foundations. These are just people hurting and exploiting others for their personal monetary benefit.

TS: Do you ever worry that you're doing what the subjects in your experiments do? That is, that you're attempting to justify a strong intuition against exploiting people, and then trying to come up with a reason why *that's* wrong—whereas maybe your intuition doesn't flash as powerfully against the veiling of women? I would think in your work that that's something you might be extremely sensitive to. How would you answer the charge that you're merely trying to come up with a reason why exploitation of different races is wrong, and veiling of women is not, without providing a sufficient basis for this judgment?

JH: That's an excellent question. Consistent with my theory, I must say that I never looked at the other side and considered whether I might be wrong in that way. We tend to think that we're right, and we're not good at coming up with reasons why we might be wrong. So that's a great question to think about, whether I am motivated to apologize for or justify some practices and not others. That said, I certainly don't think I'm motivated in that way… my first experiences in Muslim or Hindu cultures were emotionally negative, in seeing the treatment of women and the hierarchy. It took me a while to get over that. And to see that these practices offended my American sensibilities, but that I was being ethnocentric in that respect.

The women that I spoke to in India—while there was a diversity of opinion, most of them did not see it as American feminists see it; they did not see veiling as something imposed upon them, to oppress them, to deny them freedom. In contrast, most black slaves in the American South were not happy about their position. And many slave owners knew that what they were doing was wrong, or at least they were ambivalent about it. Now, you might say: Well, maybe the women have been brainwashed? So there are two tests you can do. The first is to ask: do the people who appear from the outside to be victims endorse the moral goals of the practice? The second test is: how robust is this endorsement? Even when they learn about alternative ways in other cultures, do they still endorse it? So while you might have found black slaves in the South who were so brainwashed that they accepted their status, I believe that if they heard about other countries where blacks were not enslaved, they would not insist that blacks ought to be enslaved.

TS: Okay, so then tracing it back to these four modules or bases on which moral systems are based. Because that's where you're going to provide your justification for whether we condemn other cultures or whether we can't…

JH: That's right, those are the four pillars in the air upon which we'll build our culture-specific moralities.

TS: These four pillars are a product of evolution. How do you respond to the age-old philosophical question that you can't derive an *ought* from an *is*? Darwinism gives us a *descriptive* story of why we might endorse things that come out of them. How do you get the claim "one *ought* to treat people below you kindly" out of this "don't harm people" module that's in place because of its contributions to biological fitness? That's the puzzle. Because when you do put your foot down and say that a culture ought not to act in a certain way, how are you getting that *ought* from a purely descriptive story about pillars of morality that evolved for non-moral reasons?

JH: You keep asking me to provide some kind of external justification, to go outside the system. But when I'm within the game—

TS: Not external justification... even internal, I'm just looking for any kind of justification.

JH: Well, from within the game, within our web of significance, it's wrong to hurt people.

III. DO LIBERALS HAVE AN IMPOVERISHED MORAL WORLDVIEW?

TS: Let's take a more concrete question: gay marriage. You brought this up in your talk at Dartmouth and the one I saw at Duke. You say that conservatives in America employ all four of the modules, whereas liberals only employ two. You said that liberals have an *impoverished* moral worldview, and that conservatives somehow have a richer moral life. Now, I don't know if that's just a way to shock the liberal intelligentsia...

JH: No, I meant it, although I don't mind doing a bit of shocking.

TS: You said that we as liberals have pared down our moral foundations to two modules, fairness and do-no-harm—whereas perfectly intelligent conservatives have all four modules.

JH: Exactly.

TS: So if you take gay marriage, and let's say we're not in Massachusetts—we're in Mississippi, and you have people who have the *intuition* that gay marriage is really wrong, that it's *impure*. Because they have that purity module that liberals lack. Do you want to say that in that culture that gay marriage is really *wrong*?

JH: I think it depends on the kind of society you have. I'm glad that we have a diversity of societies in this world. And some societies become experts in lives of piety and sanctity and divinity. The four modules are not virtues themselves. Virtues come out of them. America is very much about individual happiness, the right to expression, self-determination. In America you do need to point to harm that befalls victims before you can limit someone else's rights. While there's not necessarily an objective truth about whether gay marriage is right or wrong, when you look at the values and virtues that we hold dear in America, and you look at who is helped and harmed by legalizing gay marriage, if you start with a utilitarian analysis, so many people benefit from gay marriage and no one is directly harmed by gay marriage. So that in itself argues in favor of gay marriage.

On the other hand, conservative morality looks not just at effects on individuals, but at the state of the social order. The fact that acts that violate certain parts of the Bible are tolerated is disturbing to conservatives, even though they can't point to any direct harm. So I do understand the source of their opposition to it. And this is a difficult case, where it can't work out well for everyone. Somebody has to give. If we were in a Muslim country, or a Catholic country where much of social and moral life was regulated in accordance with purity and hierarchy codes, then it would be very reasonable to ban gay marriage. But we are not in such a country. We are in a country where the consensus is that we grant rights to self-determination unless a limiting reason can be found. So in this case, I think conservatives have to give. It is *right* to legalize gay marriage.

TS: I want to make sure I understood that. If we were in the 1930s—I don't want to stereotype—but 1930s Alabama, there's a pretty safe one, maybe the modules of purity and tradition played more of a role than they do now. Let's say you're the father of a man who wants to marry another man. You would feel comfortable saying to your son that it's wrong to marry—it's *wrong* for you do that.

JH: I do think that facts about the prevalence of homosexuality and the degree of repugnance to it are relevant. In the present case, 5 percent of people are gay. That's a lot of people. And in the present case, repugnance against homosexuality is not nearly as strong as it used to be. I think we are now at the point where we *ought* to legalize gay marriage, and some people just won't be happy about it. But now look at Justice Scalia's argument in opposing *Lawrence v. Texas*. Scalia's argument is very interesting. I think it's ultimately wrong, but wrong for an empirical reason. I'm paraphrasing: he said, "If we have to legalize sodomy, the next step will be incest and sex with animals." But I don't think that would be the next step. Five percent of people cannot live full happy lives if homosexuality is outlawed. If 5 percent of people could not live full happy lives without having sex with their siblings, or with sheep, then we'd have a difficult moral problem on our hands. But we don't. Very few people fall into either category. So legalizing homosexuality is not the first step on a slippery slope to legalizing everything.

TS: Okay, but getting back to my question, we're in 1930s Alabama. Five percent of the people are still gay, I imagine, but repugnance is *much* higher. Is it wrong then? Or maybe you think it's not a proper question.

JH: No, I think it's a very good question. The amount of shock and outrage would have been much greater then than it is now. Plus, back then they didn't know the facts about homosexuality; they didn't know that it's caused by hormonal conditions in utero, it's not a choice. Now that we know these facts we're in a much better position than they were then. I don't know if that answers your question.

TS: Well, maybe it does. Correct me if I'm wrong: maybe you want to say yes, in that case it probably would have been wrong. Maybe you want to say to your son: No, you ought not marry that man, or even carry on a relationship with him. *But,* given that we're not in that situation now, that's changed. Is that not a fair analysis of what the implications of your theory are?

JH: Yes, I think so. Given that there's not an objective (nonanthropo-centric) fact of the matter, and what makes our moral life so interest-ing is that any particular act can be justified or opposed by reference to a different constellation of these four modules, of these founda-tional intuitions, it really is a matter of argument, public discussion, triggering people's intuitions, and somehow or other the chips fall in a certain way. Sometimes, with time, they fall in a different way. Ten years ago, or even three years ago, we never thought that we'd be this close to having gay marriage—we have it, actually.

IV. "EVERYONE IS MORALLY MOTIVATED"

TS: Let's continue with this culture-war discussion. You tend to sound quite pessimistic about the state of affairs in America. What are the prospects of discussion between conservatives and liber-als, given that conservatives make use of two modules—purity and hierarchy—that we liberals care little about? Are we speaking dif-ferent languages? How can we get past this?

JH: First, it would help if liberals understood conservatives better. If I have a mission in life, it is to convince people that *everyone* is morally motivated—everyone except for psychopaths. Everyone else is morally motivated. Liberals need to understand that conser-vatives are motivated by more than greed and hatred. And Amer-icans and George Bush in particular need to understand that even terrorists are pursuing moral goods. One of the most psychologi-cally stupid things anyone ever said is that the 9/11 terrorists did what they did because they hate our freedom. That's just idiotic. Nobody says: "They're free over there. I hate that. I want to kill them." They did this because they hate us, they're angry at us for *many* reasons, and terrorism and violence are "moral" actions, by which I don't mean morally *right,* I mean morally motivated.

TS: And at the same time you want liberals to understand that we didn't go into Iraq just for oil or Halliburton.

JH: Of course not. Bush is Manichaean. He really believes that we are in a battle of good versus evil. Now I think that *strategically* he led us into disaster. But I never believed for a moment that this was about oil.

TS: As an aside, I completely agree with you on this. Being in an academic environment, I'm very frustrated with how people view conservatives—as moral monsters whose only goal is to pursue evil. It's a little like the pro-choice, pro-life debate, where the pro-choice faction looks at the other side as though all it wants to do is oppress women.

JH: Exactly, exactly. That's the press secretary at work; that's what he does. The press secretary doesn't just explain your actions in the best light. He strips away any *possible* moral motivation for the opponent. It's the same thing. Liberals want to understand conservatives as motivated only by greed and racism. They think that conservatives just want to hurt minorities and get money. And that completely misses the point.

TS: So what would be the consequences of everyone understanding that the other side is morally motivated? I guess we could just get down to the nuts and bolts of the issues at hand.

JH: We would become much more tolerant, and some compromise might be possible, for example, on gay marriage. Even though personally I would like to see it legalized everywhere, I think it would be a nice compromise if each state could decide whether to legalize it, and nobody was forced one way or the other by the Supreme Court. And then gay people who lived in Alabama, if they wanted to get married, could go to Massachusetts.

TS: So there are some nice social implications of your theory—if we can understand and apply it properly. I'm curious how your theory has affected you personally. There's a large element of self-deception that's involved in moral judgment, according to your model.

JH: That's right.

TS: So I'm curious how that's affected *you* in your day-to-day life. Are you more distrustful of moral judgments that you make? Do you find yourself questioning your own motives or beliefs, or do you not take your work home with you?

JH: Well, for one thing, I am more tolerant of others. I was *much* more tolerant of Republicans and conservatives until the last two years. George Bush and his administration have got me so angry that I find my hard-won tolerance fast disappearing. I am now full of anger. And I find my press secretary drawing up the brief against Bush and his administration. So I can say that doing this work, coming up with this theory, has given me insight into what I'm doing. When I fulminate, my press secretary writes a brief against Bush. Once passions come into play, reason follows along. At least now I know that I'm doing it.

TS: Do you say to yourself: Wait a minute, reason is the press secretary of my emotions—I now have reason to distrust this anger?

JH: I don't do that.

TS: Do you think you should?

JH: No. Because I don't think there's an objective truth of the matter.[3] Also, outrage is fun. Outrage is pleasurable. I'm enjoying my outrage.

TS: Okay, then let's bring this back full circle. What do you think

---

[3] Upon reflection a few months later, Haidt agreed that he should question his anger, and that his response here was a post hoc justification of his anger.

of Julie and Mark and their consensual sex in the south of France? Is it wrong?

JH: It's fine with me. Doesn't bother me in the least. Remember: I'm a liberal. So if it doesn't involve harm to someone, it's not a big deal to me. Liberals love to find victims, and incest cases are usually ones in which someone is being harmed. But that's the trick of the question. They're both adults, and it's consensual. So liberals have an especially hard time trying to justify why it's wrong. But I wrote the story, so I know the trick. ✶

8

STEPHEN STICH

"I WALK THE LINE."

O f all the stereotypes about philosophers, perhaps the most durable is the one about how we spend our days in armchairs, content to expound about the laws of the universe, gazes securely affixed to navels. (Sometimes there's a pipe and a tweed jacket with elbow patches thrown into the mix as well.) The idea behind this picture is that there's a sharp distinction between philosophers on the one hand, and scientists—those people who think you actually have to leave your armchairs and observe the world if you're going to learn anything about it—on the other. Like many stereotypes, this one contains more than a kernel of truth; indeed, many philosophers would embrace it. But there are and always have been exceptions: philosophers who have devoted their careers to blurring or obliterating the line between philosophical and scientific inquiry. Stephen Stich—Board of Governors

Professor at Rutgers University—is perhaps the most prominent contemporary example of this kind of philosopher. Beginning with his groundbreaking work on cross-cultural diversity in beliefs about knowledge and truth, and continuing with his more recent work in ethics, Stich has revealed the vital importance of taking an empirically informed approach to age-old philosophical problems.

Bringing science into philosophy may not seem all that controversial, but many philosophers treat this idea as pure poison. No area in the field generates as much hostility. Philosophers are part of the academy, after all, and will go to great lengths to defend their turf. But after publishing four books and a list of articles far too numerous to mention, as well as winning several prestigious lifetime-achievement awards in philosophy, Stich has been able to carve a place for empirically informed philosophy from the inside of the academic establishment. As much as anyone else in the world right now, Stich has made working on the vague boundary between philosophy and science a respectable endeavor, something you can get paid to do. For this, many young philosophers will forever be in his debt.

Our interview took place in the park outside of the Minneapolis Museum of Art, and then in the coffee shop upstairs. After talking about empirically informed philosophy in general, our discussion turned to how this approach sheds light on crucial problems in ethics. The view that emerges is not quite moral relativism, not quite moral nihilism or skepticism, but something stranger and harder to pin down.

May 2008

I. EXPERIMENTAL PHILOSOPHY: A CONTRADICTION IN TERMS?

TAMLER SOMMERS: You came to my university this spring for our lecture series, and gave a talk called "Why Experimental Philosophers Are Not Oxymorons." First, what is experimental philosophy, exactly?

STEPHEN STICH: Well, there's an important sense in which experimental philosophy is a very old idea. If you go back to the seventeenth and eighteenth centuries, the great philosophical figures of that period were not only informed about the empirical sciences but in many cases contributed to the empirical sciences. Descartes, Berkeley, and many others. That's a tradition that has waxed and waned over the centuries. It certainly hasn't been popular in the second half of the twentieth century. As I conceive of it—and many other people have different accounts—experimental philosophy is simply using experimental and more broadly scientific techniques and methods to answer questions that are important in philosophical discussion and debate.

TS: Can you give an example?

SS: Sure. Characterized in that way, lots of nonphilosophers do experimental philosophy. My favorite example is the work of Daniel Batson who, as I see it, is one of the great experimental philosophers. He's interested in the traditional debate that goes all the way back to Hobbes, some would say all the way back to Plato, about whether human beings can be *genuinely* altruistic. Batson has designed experiments to try to demonstrate that the answer is yes. In doing this, he's addressing a traditional philosophical question, a debate that's really quite central in ethics, using experimental means.

TS: Do you have a favorite of these experiments that you can describe?

SS: Batson's strategy is to divide and conquer. The debate in this area is between those who believe in human altruism on the one hand and the "psychological egoists" on the other. Psychological egoists are people who say that of course human beings *help* other people—no one has seriously denied that—people help each other even at a cost to themselves. But the deep question is: what is their motive? The psychological egoists say that their motive is always self-interested in one way or another. Batson's strategy is to look at each of the traditional self-interested explanations of helping behavior and try to design experiments where you pit an altruistic explanation and an egoistic explanation against each other. The goal is to design experiments that will enable you to rule out one or the other. Perhaps his most famous series of experiments looks at one egoist idea, a particularly popular one, both traditionally, going all the way back to Hobbes, and also in the contemporary literature, particularly in the social sciences. He gives this idea an unfortunate name: "the aversive-arousal reduction hypothesis."

TS: Unfortunate, to say the least...

SS: Batson is a great psychologist but his nomenclature leaves something to be desired. What this unfortunate name refers to is the egoistic hypothesis that says you help people because seeing their distress, being aware of their distress, causes *you* to be distressed. And your motive in helping people, the deep motive, the underlying motive, is to alleviate your own distress—your "aversive-arousal."

TS: It's worth helping people so that you can stop feeling their pain.

SS: Yes. So, simplifying a little bit, Batson set up situations in which an experimental participant can either help someone or simply leave. And he manipulates whether it's easy or hard to leave. The idea here is if you're genuinely altruistically motivated, if your ultimate motivation is to help the target person, the person who needs the help, then you should help whether leaving is easy or hard.

TS: How was all this measured—by whether it was easy or hard to leave?

SS: Well, let me describe the situation. In one famous experiment, participants *believe*—there's a certain amount of deception here—they *believe* they're seeing another participant over closed-circuit TV. (It's actually a video tape.) And they believe that their job is to watch and evaluate the other participant as she does a learning experiment that requires her to get mild electric shocks. But she's having evident distress at the electric shocks, though they're supposed to be relatively mild. She explains to the experimenter that because of a childhood trauma, she is particularly sensitive to relatively mild electric shocks, and so she's finding this really distressing. Then the experimenter on the tape says, "Okay, well maybe the other participant (who is the real experimental subject here) would be willing to change places with you." At this point, the tape stops, and the real experimental subject is asked whether he or she would be willing to change places with the person being shocked. The manipulation on "easy to escape" versus "hard to escape" is that in one case, the subjects are told that if they choose not to change places with the other participant, then they are free to go. The other group of people are told, "Well, if you choose not to change places with the woman getting the shocks, then you have to continue the experiment and watch eight more trials." So they would have to watch her getting shocked a number of additional times. Now, suppose you're motivated by "aversive-arousal reduction"—that is to say, the desire to stop the unpleasant reaction you're having because you see this other person getting shocked. If that's your motivation, then in one experimental condition you can simply walk out and not have to worry about that anymore. However, if you have to endure eight more trials of watching the person get shocked, then, well...

TS: You'd be more motivated to switch places, according to the egoistic theory.

SS: Right. And so what happens is—it's slightly complicated—there's another manipulation to affect the extent to which the participant empathizes with the person being shocked. Batson's hypothesis is that you do get real altruism, but only in high-empathy conditions. And in fact participants in the high-empathy condition did agree to switch places with the person getting shocked, whether leaving was easy or hard.

TS: Whether or not they would have to stay and watch more shocks.

SS: Yes. So I think that Batson's work really does move the ego-ism versus altruism debate forward, which is why it's my parade case for the success of experimental philosophy. You can find the aversive-arousal reduction hypothesis—not under that horrible la-bel, of course—in Hobbes. People have been debating the idea for centuries, and there hasn't been much progress! And here's Batson saying, Look, this doesn't establish that we are genuinely altruistic, of course, but it does establish that if you pit altruism against this particular version of the egoistic hypothesis, this egoistic hypothe-sis turns out to be untenable; it's not what's happening.

II. "LARGE PARTS OF WHAT PHILOSOPHERS HAVE DONE ARE NOT WORTH DOING."

TS: All this sounds wonderful. So why, in your judgment, have philosophers been so resistant—hostile, really—to experimental or empirically informed approaches to our subject?

SS: Good question, and I'm sure I can't give you a complete an-swer. You're certainly right about the hostility out there. I think that there are a couple of factors that can partially explain it. The first is suggested by one of my favorite quotes, a passage in "Fin de siè-cle Ethics," which is an essay written by three of the most eminent moral theorists of our time, Allan Gibbard, Peter Railton, and Ste-phen Darwall. In the passage that I particularly like, they say that too many philosophers—and parenthetically they add "We don't ex-empt ourselves"—are content to simply *invent* the facts when they need factual claims to buttress their philosophical arguments. Think about this for a moment: it's a very shocking observation. Philos-ophers—and I think this was particularly rampant in the last fifty years of the previous century, and still to a very considerable extent in this century—philosophers have gotten into a pattern of simply declaring various sorts of things to be the case, things that are clearly empirical matters, *without a shred of evidence for it!* There's something deeply intellectually disreputable about simply inventing the facts.

TS: So philosophers see this movement as a threat to their unrespectable habits?

SS: Well, the contrast is that the experimental philosophers are standing off to the side saying, "Look, if you're going to make an empirical claim, particularly one that it isn't obviously true, you need some *evidence*. Inventing the facts is not a respectable activity. In many other areas of the academic world, inventing the facts would get you fired! *Disreputable* is a very mild term for it. This practice of making claims about the nature of human motivation, or about what all people would agree to, or about what people think, and pulling these facts—these putative facts—out of thin air is really something of an intellectual disgrace.

TS: But in their own minds, they're not saying, "Hey, these experimental philosophers are preventing us from continuing our disgraceful practices!" Right? So this would have to be sort of an unconscious motive for the hostility, no?

SS: Perhaps, perhaps. One of my favorites quotes is from Newton, who said "*hypotheses non fingo*"—I don't feign hypotheses. In this area, I'm just not at all sure what people are thinking. But work in experimental philosophy certainly poses a threat to those traditions in philosophy where people make clearly factual claims with no evidence. Now, I said there were two reasons that I could come up with for the controversial nature of the experimental approach. One is that it underscores the lamentable practice of inventing empirical facts to suit your theory. The other is that some of us, some experimental philosophers—and I suppose I've been one of the principal offenders—some of us have suggested that findings in experimental philosophy undermine a *major* methodology that philosophers have been using for a very long time. Arguably, this methodology goes all the way back to Socrates or Plato. It's the method of supporting philosophical theories by using intuitions.

TS: Where intuitions means...

SS: Well, of course it's complicated and controversial, but to simplify a bit: an intuition is a spontaneous judgment about whether a particular case should be classified in one way or another. So going back to Plato, it's a judgment about whether a particular case counts as an instance of justice or an instance of piety, or in the contemporary literature, it's asking whether a person in a specified situation really has knowledge of something or not. The method of attempting to capture the intuitions and supporting your theory on the basis of these intuitions is a venerable one in philosophy. It's not the only method, but it's one of the most central and most widely used methods. Now, what I've been arguing for a long time actually, and have recently begun backing up empirically, is that this entire tradition rests on a very problematic bet. It's a bet that until recently hasn't been acknowledged. It's the bet that there isn't substantial *variation* in philosophically important intuitions. In particular, that there is no cross-cultural variation.

TS: Philosophers are assuming that these intuitions are universally shared?

SS: Well, "universally" may be too strong. But they are betting that there is not a lot of cross-cultural variation. Even many proponents of this method, like my colleague Ernie Sosa, concede that if there is indeed significant intergroup variation in these intuitions— whether there is an empirical question and a hard one—then the use of these intuitions in philosophy—this whole methodology— is undermined. And if that's the case, if philosophers lose their bet, what I've been arguing is that a vast amount of what philosophers have done recently, but also going all the way back to antiquity, belongs in the rubbish bin.

So not surprisingly—if the question is Why do people get their backs up about experimental philosophy—that might be a principal reason. If in fact intuitions are culturally variable, or vary by socioeconomic status, or vary in other kinds of ways, then many sorts of philosophical theories based on intuition simply are not to be trusted, and large parts of what philosophers have done are not worth doing.

TS: So for many philosophers, experimental philosophy poses a challenge not just to their own methodology, but to the history of philosophy, or at least large sections of it. I can see how that would arouse a bit of ill will.

SS: Yes. Another thing I've said—perhaps unwisely—is that philosophers typically use the doubly dubious technique of basing their theories on *their own* intuitions along with (as Alison Gopnik[1] once put it) the intuitions of the six white guys down the hall. But until very recently there has been no serious attempt to justify the technique—perhaps none since Plato. Plato at least had a theory to justify this technique. It was his theory of recollection, which says that our souls knew the truth before we were born, and that we forgot most of it when our souls got trapped in our bodies. So intuition is just a sort of recollection. Now I've never met anyone who took this theory seriously. I'm not sure Plato took it seriously. But at least he had the intellectual honesty to present a theory to justify the technique. In the time since Plato, almost no one has tried to give a theory to tell us why we should rely on intuition—why this is a good thing to do—until the last few years, when Tim Williamson, Ernie Sosa, and others have tried to address the issue. For centuries, philosophers have been basing their theories on intuition without ever having asked why that's a legitimate thing to do. So for 2,400 years we've had a methodology that had no justification. The thrust of recent work in experimental philosophy is that there are important cross-cultural and interpersonal differences in intuition. And if that's right, then providing a justification for this sort of "intuition mongering" will be much harder. I want to stress that the evidence we now have is far from conclusive; but most of the straws in the wind are pointing in the same direction. And if there are significant demographic differences in intuition, then the method of basing philosophical theories on intuition may have to be thrown out.

---

[1] Gopnik is a professor of psychology and affiliate professor of philosophy at UC Berkeley.

III. TAKING ON MORAL REALISM

TS: Of course, this challenge has serious implications for theories about the nature of knowledge and the proper way to acquire it. But I should move on to how empirical work in the sciences bears on issues in ethics. (Although of course these notions are related.) Many of your recent articles argue that work in the sciences undermines the metaethical theory of "moral realism."[2] First, for the nonphilosophers out there, and maybe some of the philosophers, too, what exactly is moral realism?

SS: The term "moral realism" is used in many different ways. As I use it, it is a label for a family of theories. What they have in common is the view that moral judgments or moral beliefs are either true or false, correct or incorrect, and that some moral beliefs at least are true. My work has focused on a subset of moral realists, who argue that we should expect *convergence* or agreement in moral judgment under some type of idealized condition, like full agreement over relevant *nonmoral* facts. So for example, you and I might disagree about a moral matter if we disagree on a factual matter; we might disagree on the right policy for dealing with global warming if we also disagree about what's causing global warming. One important group of moral realists, which includes many of the moral theorists associated with Cornell University, believe that if you were to completely eliminate all factual disagreement, you'd eliminate most moral disagreement as well.

TS: To take another example, over something like gay marriage, these theorists would say that once all the relevant facts were known—the effects of gay marriage on heterosexual marriage, for example, or the effects on children, and maybe some religious issues too—then there would no longer be disagreement over whether it was morally right to allow people of the same sex to marry. And accord-

---

[2] Chapters 4 (Michael Ruse), 6 (Joshua Greene and Liane Young), and 7 (Jonathan Haidt) feature more discussion on moral realism versus moral skepticism and relativism.

ing to these theorists, whatever everyone would agree upon under these idealized conditions is morally right, objectively speaking. It's the morally *correct* view.

SS: Yes, right. The central idea is that morality is in some important ways analogous to science. In science, one expects there to be plenty of disagreement on the hard questions, but one also expects convergence over time on an increasingly large number of issues. That, of course, is what we've seen in disciplines like astronomy, chemistry, and biology, and it's what moral realists expect in morality as well. And it's here that I think that the empirical evidence is crucially important. Because what my collaborators and I have been arguing is that this isn't true. Our view is that of course you'd eliminate *some* moral disagreement if you eliminated factual disagreement, but there would still be a great deal of moral disagreement left, because moral disagreement does not arise only from disagreement over nonmoral facts. So these are the targets that we have taken aim at, these so-called "convergentist moral realists." We think that empirical work tends to undermine the claim that convergentists make, although of course the issue is far from settled.

TS: Can you give a good example of where empirical work has undermined the idea that moral views would converge under idealized circumstances?

SS: Well, I think the focus has to be on an empirically supported theory about what moral judgments are *like*. That theory has to specify what the psychological mechanisms underlying moral judgments are; it also has to provide both a developmental and an evolutionary account of why we have those psychological mechanisms. Obviously, a theory of that sort will be very complex. No single experiment or empirical observation could come close to establishing such a theory. And since it is the theory that poses the greatest challenge to moral realism, no single experiment can undermine moral realism. At best, individual studies can lend support to the theory, or to aspects of the theory.

TS: Without going into the kind of detail that would take up the rest of our time, can you describe this theory that you believe undermines moral realism of this kind?

SS: That's a tall order! The work supporting it is drawn from a lot a different areas, some of it exploring cross-cultural differences in moral judgments that don't look like they can be easily explained by differences in factual judgment.

TS: Maybe start with an example of some that work?

SS: Well, one nice example emerged in work that I have been doing in collaboration with John Doris, Kaiping Peng, and others on moral dilemmas like "the Magistrate and the Mob." As you know, the problem posed in the Magistrate and the Mob is whether the judge and the chief of police in a town should falsely accuse and convict an innocent person in order to prevent a mob from rioting and causing a lot of damage and suffering to the townspeople.

TS: This is the scenario philosophers use to pit the utilitarian principle (go with action that produces that greatest good for the greatest number) against the Kantian or deontological principle that you should never knowingly punish an innocent person, no matter how much good it will lead to.

SS: Yes, and the evidence indicates that there is a quite dramatic cross-cultural difference between Chinese and American people on these kinds of issues.

TS: The Chinese come to the more utilitarian conclusion that it's okay to convict an innocent person in order to prevent the rioting. And the Americans don't.

SS: Yes, although that's not to say they're more utilitarian. They just happen to agree with the utilitarian here. We suspect that the real explanation is that they are more communitarian. Of course, with any given result, one could worry that there is some sort of factual assumption in the background on which the two groups differ, but we argue that this is unlikely to be the case here or in a number of other cases that have been studied. What's much more likely to be the case is that there is a difference in the underlying system of norms that is more *community*-focused in Chinese culture, and more *individually* focused in the American case.

TS: And therefore that greater knowledge about other facts, or improved rationality of some kind, wouldn't resolve this moral disagreement.

SS: Yes, though that requires a considerable leap from data to theory. It would be preposterous to make that leap based on a small number of studies. But what I've tried to do, in collaboration with Chandra Sripada, is assemble a body of data from the literature in anthropology, psychology, neuroscience, experimental economics, and several other domains, to support a theory which claims that a special-purpose part of the human mind is designed to detect and store socially salient norms.

TS: Could you describe what a norm is on this account?

SS: Norms, as we conceive of them, are mentally represented rules specifying how people should or should not behave. They serve to trigger emotions and moral judgments—probably the emotions play a very important role in the production of the judgments. So the crucial bit here is that there is a component of the mind which is in one respect like the language faculty. (Only in one respect, let me stress.) It's an innate part of the mind whose function is to acquire information from the environment and to store it and use it. And we believe that, as in the case of language, once those rules are in place, it is very hard to dislodge them. In particular, learning a bunch of facts is not going to do it. So, to use a crude analogy, when you learned English as a child you internalized a set of rules in the part of the mind devoted to storing language competence. You can learn facts until you're a very old man, but that won't stop you from being an English speaker. Similarly, we claim, once you take on board the norms of the surrounding culture, there are no facts you can learn that will get those norms out of the part of the mind devoted to storing norms.

TS: And these norms are different across cultures, developed as responses to different parts of the social and physical environment.

SS: Absolutely.

TS: So to continue with the crude analogy, would you say that just as it's not more rational or more objectively correct to speak English rather than Chinese—it just depends on the environment you're in—in the same way, there's nothing more rational or objectively correct about having a certain kind of moral belief or moral judgment?

SS: Well, the view is potentially inflammatory and therefore needs to be stated with care. But on the model that Sripada and I develop, it looks to me that the appropriate thing to say about norms and moral judgments is that *they aren't the kinds of things that are correct or incorrect, true or false.* But the crucial point I want to make is that even if by using some clever philosophical tools you could develop an argument to show that moral claims can be true, that some norms are correct and some norms aren't, in an important sense that's neither here nor there. Remember, the moral realist we're focusing on is the one who says that if we just get more rational or learn some new nonmoral facts, then our moral views will converge. And my contention is that this isn't true. The norms you've taken on board are different from those that have been internalized by people in different cultures, and they lead you to make different moral judgments. Those judgments are not likely to converge no matter how many additional facts you learn. So when people in different groups have internalized very different norms, it is very likely that we're stuck with deep moral disagreement.

TS: But now there are two ways of looking at that claim. The first is that certain people, certain cultures, are stuck having false or pernicious moral views. Just like color-blind people are stuck not being able to see the redness of a rose. And that unfortunately there's nothing we can do about it. But the rose is still red. The second is that there *is no fact of the matter* about whether any particular moral belief is true or false. Assuming your work does undermine the type of realist you're targeting, would there be some other way of establishing the truth of moral claims?

SS: That's not a question that admits of a simple answer, since there are lots of ways in which a moral realist might try to establish that some moral claims are true. Some moral realists offer rather surprising and implausible accounts of the *meaning* of moral claims; others develop novel accounts of *truth*. There is plenty of logical and philosophical space for moral realists to explore. But I'm not sanguine about any of these strategies.

TS: Are there other *plausible* ways of establishing the truth of moral claims?

SS: No, I think not.

IV. ARE MORAL JUDGMENTS LIKE CHICHA JUDGMENTS?

TS: So it seems like you're arriving at a kind of moral relativism, which I agree is inflammatory. But, well, the fact that a view is inflammatory doesn't make it false. If a theory is true, it's true— whether op-ed columnists like it or not. So would you characterize the "metaethical" view (as philosophers call it) that you find most plausible as a relativist one? That is, the view that no moral judgment can be true or false objectively, universally, across all cultures?

SS: Well, I don't like to call it moral relativism; I much prefer to call it antirealism. The reason for that is that moral relativists tend to think a given judgment can be correct for one culture and incorrect for another. Whereas my kind of antirealism says no, it's not that judgments can be true in one culture but not in another culture. *None* of them is correct, no matter what culture you're in. So that's why I don't like to call it relativism. In some sense it's more radical than relativism. My view is that norms and the moral judgments to which they lead aren't in the *business* of being true or false.

TS: People certainly seem to *think* that moral judgments can be true, though, right?

SS: Well, it is clear that *some* people think that; certainly some philosophers do. But I don't think we know how widespread this belief is. I've been doing some thinking about this since you sent me your list of questions. I think a really nice analogy, and maybe a psychologically important one, too, is to certain emotions. One particularly useful example is disgust. Commonsensically, people think certain activities or foods are disgusting. My tastes run fairly low on the disgust scale: relatively few things disgust me. But one of the things that does is a South American beverage called *chicha*. Chicha is a fermented beverage, a bit like beer, prepared using human spit. What am I inclined to think about chicha? Well, I think it's disgusting. And the phenomenology, how it appears to me, is that the disgustingness is *something about the chicha*. I'm just detecting it. But of course, the people for whom this is a favorite beverage find nothing disgusting about it. So let's look more closely at this. Is it plausible that they're wrong and I'm right? Is there something they're missing here? Are these South Americans just confused somehow, unaware of how disgusting chicha is? Well, no, that's not what's going on, in spite of the fact that it seems to me that there's something objectively disgusting about chicha.

TS: So we're projecting our own disgust on to the chicha.

SS: Yes. Actually, there are two parts of the story. The first goes back to Hume. Our minds project, they paint various things on the world, and disgustingness is one of those things. The human mind makes some things in the world appear disgusting. And it's very hard to get our heads around the fact that chicha, or a baby's pooey diaper, aren't objectively disgusting. The second part of the story comes from the sciences—particularly psychology and anthropology. They find that there is a great deal of cross-cultural variation in what people take to be disgusting. Moreover, there are processes that increasingly we're beginning to understand, which underlie the acquisition of disgust elicitors (or "triggers"), and in many cases those triggers are culturally local. The cultural variation and the processes underlying it make it clear that when we find something disgusting we are not detecting anything objective in the world. That's why I think disgust judgments are a useful analogy for moral judgments. Yes indeed, moral judgments present themselves to us as saying something about the world. Then we do some science on our own judgments and the mechanisms underlying them, and on the cross-cultural facts about the phenomena, and it turns out that the best science tells us that moral judgments are not detecting objective features of the world. If you and an Ecuadorian disagree about the disgustingness of chicha, there's nothing that's going to settle that disagreement. And similarly for moral disagreements.

TS: Okay, that's a very nice analogy for your view, but there seems to be something different between taste judgments and moral judgments—I had a similar discussion with Jon Haidt about this issue. I might find chicha to be completely nasty, but as soon as I learn that Ecuadorians love it, I'm happy to agree that there's no right or wrong answer about whether or not it's disgusting. In spite of that perceptual experience you talk about, people are more or less willing to be antirealists about taste judgments. By contrast, people are much more resistant to antirealism about moral judgments. Take the examples of genital mutilations or honor killings. Americans think these practices are morally wrong. And even when they learn that these are practices that run deep into the heart of other cultures, that these cultures don't see the issue in the same way we do, the reaction isn't, "Well, okay, let's agree to disagree." In this case, unlike the chicha case, we think honor killings or genital mutilation are objectively wrong. We think the people who perform those practices have false moral beliefs. Why would there be that extra bit of resistance when it comes to morality?

SS: Well here I would accuse you of doing what philosophers do rather too much, which is pull facts out of thin air.

TS: A nice way of describing the place I'm pulling facts out of....

SS: Well, it's far from clear that people *do* react to disagreement in the way you describe, either on the disgust side or the moral side. Nor is it clear that everyone reacts in the same way.

TS: So you don't think that people are more resistant to antirealism about morality than they are to antirealism about taste?

SS: I guess I just don't know what the answer to that question is. It seems to me to be very much an empirical question about which we have precious little evidence.

TS: I'd agree that it's an empirical question. But even the phrase "it's a matter of taste"—that's a metaphor for antirealism, isn't it? That's what people say when they concede that there's no fact of the matter about a certain question.

SS: Well, look: even if it turns out that you're right—and this seems to me to be something that would be intriguing to explore empirically—there might be a range of reasons for that. It may be that the norm system plays an importantly different role and perhaps a much more pervasive role in people's lives than the disgust system. After all, the norm system plays a hugely important role in characterizing *who you take yourself to be*. Disgust plays some role in that, but not nearly as important a role. And there's the issue of motivation as well. Disgust can certainly motivate us, especially when it comes to avoidance. The norm system motivates us to avoid things too, but in addition the norm system can lead sometimes, not always, to punitive motivation.

TS: Actually, I'd like to talk about that. When I interviewed Michael Ruse, he argued that the evolutionary function of moral norms, moral judgments, requires that we see them objectively. In his view, the norms wouldn't function as effectively to motivate adaptive behavior—like punitive behavior—if we didn't see them as corresponding to something objective. Whereas with disgust, if you find something disgusting, that's enough motivation for you to avoid it. You don't need to see it as objectively disgusting. Whereas when we're talking about doing something immoral but very tempting, there might not be enough motivation for you to refrain from doing it unless you thought it was objectively wrong. So maybe that's where the persistent illusion of objectivity lies, in the function of these moral norms and judgments.

SS: I'd be hesitant to endorse that story for two reasons, both of them empirical. First of all, we certainly are far from having a conclusive story about why the norm system evolved. There's plenty of debate about the evolutionary function of this system, assuming the system exists. Another empirical question is: would realizing the nature of the psychology that underlies norms undermine part of your motivation to act on your norms? Here again, the answer is far from clear.

TS: In other words, you're wondering whether understanding the psychology of our norm system, and therefore believing norms not to be objective, would have any effect on our motivation whatsoever.

SS: Right. Thinking about the question makes it clear that there may be real implications of a practical sort in more deeply understanding moral psychology. If the answer is yes—if losing the sense of objectivity would undermine your motivation to act according to norms—that's something to think about when promulgating this view. But it strikes as me as far from clear that this is the case. Let's think about disgust. I know a fair amount about the psychology of disgust and how disgust judgments vary across cultures. Does that in any way diminish my avoidance of the things I find disgusting? In most cases, not at all. Certainly my reluctance to drink chicha is not in any way diminished by my understanding that there's nothing objective about its disgustingness. Why not? Well, look, you can understand how something works, but it still works. Okay, now what about norms? You raise questions about genital mutilation, or practices in honor cultures, and it seems to me that I can perfectly well be an antirealist from the theoretical perspective, and say that my norms are not more objectively correct than those of an honor culture person. Or suppose I disagree with someone about a political issue like gay marriage, or the appropriate role of women in society. Here again, taking the theoretical perspective, I can be an antirealist and insist that their norms are neither more true nor less true than mine. Norms are just not in that business. Nonetheless, I'm *deeply wedded* to my norms; they play a large role in making me who I am. And in this respect I'm not at all unhappy about who I am. So am I motivated to act on those norms? Yes. Will I act on them? You bet I will!

V. CAN MORAL INTERVENTION BE JUSTIFIED? (AND DOES IT NEED TO BE JUSTIFIED?)

TS: You say you'll act on your norms. Will you do this even to the point of preventing other people from acting on *their* norms?

SS: Well, of course, not everything I take to be morally wrong is something I'm prepared to try to force people to stop. But in cases like genital mutilation or certain other kinds of treatment of women, the answer is most definitely yes. I recognize that other people have other norms, that there's nothing objective about theirs or mine, but I will still work very hard to try to stop them from engaging in these practices.

TS: But think how inappropriate it would be to go on a campaign, to go on some misguided mission to stop people in Ecuador from drinking chicha. There would be something wrong with that, right? They like chicha, they enjoy it. Let them drink their chicha. Now you used that same analogy for moral judgments—why wouldn't you feel that it's deeply inappropriate for people to be campaigning against genital mutilation or other practices arising from different norms?

SS: The answer there, it seems to me, turns on the differences between disgust psychology and norm psychology. And perhaps the differences in their functions, insofar as we understand anything about their functions. Why? Well, because in the case of norms, in addition to there being compliance motivation, there is also motivation to punish people who are norm violators. And this isn't part of the disgust system. So the psychological systems work differently. That's not surprising, since they evolved for different purposes. So you're quite right that if I find out that someone enjoys chicha I'm not inclined to prevent him from or to punish him for drinking it. But the norm system works differently. We *are* inclined to prevent people from violating norms and to punish them when they violate norms. So again, I'm inclined as a theoretician to say: here's how it works. But, of course, that system is still part of me. And I'm perfectly happy with this norm system being part of me. Now I concede that I might be wrong about the disconnect between psychological knowledge and moral motivation. It could turn out that if you think about the psychology of norms long enough or hard enough, that could undermine your motivation to punish norm violators and prevent people from violating your norms. But I don't see why that would happen.

TS: But it's not *just* a question of what we're inclined to do, right? There's also the question of what's *appropriate* to do. And—correct me if I'm wrong—you said that different norm systems have evolved in response to different kinds of environments. So isn't there something deeply inappropriate about converting other people in different environments and therefore with different norms to our value system?

SS: There's a lot packed into that question, so let me start by doing some unpacking. First of all, you've changed the focus a bit by asking about *converting* other people to our value system. It is far from clear to me that this is possible. As I noted earlier, I think the norm system may be a bit like the language system: once a rule is internalized, it may be *very* difficult to change. But now, what about trying to change people's behavior, or punishing them for norm violations? In addition to having norms regulating certain sorts of behavior, we also have norms governing what to do about various sorts of norm violations. So there are things that, if I learn that you've done them, I might condemn you for doing. But a very different issue is whether I should try to stop you from doing these things or whether the state should try to stop you. Those are separate normative questions.

TS: I agree with that, certainly.

SS: For example, suppose I learn that you have been mean to your maiden aunt who took care of you for twenty years. You are not exhibiting the sort of gratitude and concern for her well-being that I think would be appropriate in those circumstances. I think you shouldn't behave that way; you're violating a norm requiring gratitude. If you are a casual acquaintance, I would probably do nothing at all. If you are my friend, I might try to persuade you to change your behavior. But I don't think I should try to force you to behave differently, nor do I think that the state should have laws against ingratitude.

TS: Okay, I agree with that. But what seems to me to be an implication of your view—I guess you don't agree—it seems like considerably more actions would fall into that second category, actions we disapprove of but shouldn't take steps to prevent. It seems inappropriate to punish people for what *you* find to be immoral behavior, because you have to think: maybe they're responding to norms that came out of *their* social and physical environment, and these norms work for them. And since there's no objective fact of the matter about whether their behavior or practice is right or wrong, why would I want to, why *should* I want to, prevent or punish them from doing it? Yes, I understand that my norms, given my environment, lead me to *want* to condemn and in some cases punish those violators, but what possible *justification* could there be for me to prevent people from responding to their norms and engaging in what our norms deem to be immoral practices?

SS: So you're suggesting that if you're an antirealist about morality, there are a variety of arguments you could not give to justify enforcing your own moral view or acting to punish people who violate your values or norms.

TS: Yes…

SS: Well, that's right. There are a variety of such arguments that you could no longer use. But now let me raise a further question: To what extent do those arguments and justifications play a significant role in people's motivations? I'm inclined to think that in our culture they play at most a very limited role, and that in many other cultures they play no role at all. These are empirical claims, of course, and they need much more systematic study. But there are a number of findings that encourage my skepticism about the role of justificatory arguments. The most famous of these is Jon Haidt's work on moral dumbfounding [see Chapter 7]. What Haidt finds is that in at least some cases involving consensual incest, people's justifications play *no role whatsoever* in the formation of their own judgments. Jon doesn't go on to ask his participants whether there should be laws against incest of this sort, but I'm willing to bet that most of them would say that laws against consensual incest were fine, that it's a good thing for the state to prohibit this sort of behavior.

TS: Even in the case of Julie and Mark, where it was consensual, they were happy with it, and the subjects couldn't justify why it was wrong. They would still say there should be a law against it.

SS: Yes, exactly. For many people, the fact that they couldn't come up with justifications wouldn't prevent them from saying that the behavior should be prohibited. Another source of evidence comes from anthropologists who have told me over and over again that when you ask people in small-scale societies to provide justifications for behaving in accordance with their norms, the standard response is: "That's what we do." They don't *have* a justification, they don't care that they don't have one. They're not even sure what you're asking for.

TS: That's really interesting.

SS: One more analogy—again only a crude analogy—is the Müller-Lyer illusion. You know that the lines in the Müller-Lyer illusion are exactly the same length, but they still look different:

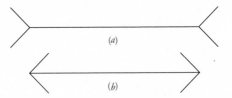

The analogy I'm suggesting is this: empirically it might be the case that you can know the psychology behind different norm systems—yours, say, or those of a culture-of-honor person—and at the theoretical level you know that there's nothing objectively better about your norm system than theirs. *But that doesn't have much of an effect at all!* You're still motivated to stop them.

TS: Okay, but let me keep playing devil's advocate here. In my interview with Haidt, my last question was: What do you think about

Julie and Mark [the incestuous brother and sister]? Was it okay for them to have sex? And he said, "Sure, I'm fine with it." Maybe knowing the psychology behind his model led him to alter his moral judgment. In fact, he said that his model had this kind of practical implication. He said it made him more tolerant of other viewpoints, other political viewpoints. He was influenced to stop trying to impose his own judgments on others, and he was less angry when people disagreed with him. And that was the very result of learning about his moral psychology.

SS: Yes, well, with all due respect to Jon, I'm not sure I believe him. After all, if cognitive science has taught us anything, it's that we are not very good at explaining the causes of our own judgments and attitudes, nor are we very good at explaining why our judgments and attitudes change.

TS: What about Bush? The justification for the Iraq War was often couched in terms of giving the gift of democratic values and freedom to the Iraqi people, and that was how the war was sold in many circles. If I understand your view correctly, if the knowledge of your view was widely disseminated, you couldn't use that kind of justification. That Americans have the right way to live—democracy for everyone.

SS: I'm not sure I follow you. What I've been claiming is that, as a matter of psychological fact, someone could make those moral judgments about the war without thinking that there is some objective way of settling his disagreement with someone who disagreed with him.

TS: How?

SS: Let's consider another example, one that isn't fraught with political considerations. I saw an excellent movie the other night called *Water*, by Deepa Mehta. It takes place in India in 1938. It's about the plight of widows in India who, if they didn't jump on the funeral pyres of their husbands, were required to live apart in widows' ashrams where they supported themselves by begging; some of them were reduced to prostitution. Some of the women in these ashrams were widowed when they were five or six years old, because child marriage was common. At the end of the movie, there's a scrolling text telling the viewer that there are still many hundreds of thousands or maybe millions of widows in India who endure conditions like the ones depicted. On my view, this is obviously another way of life—another "form of life," as the Wittgensteinians might say. However, it's a form that I take to be bad, and in saying that, I'm making a moral judgment. I think it should change! You might ask: Suppose there's someone who has internalized the cluster of the norms that sustain the widows' ashram system and makes that form of life possible. He (or she!) acquired those norms from his culture just as I acquired most of my norms from my culture. In this case, is there something objectively correct about my norms and incorrect about his? My answer is no.

TS: But then why do you say it *should* change? I guess I don't see what allows you to say that.

SS: I'm not sure what the question means. Why do I have to be allowed?

TS: In the same way that if I said "Chicha's disgusting," you would say, "Well, disgusting to *you.*"

SS: No no, I wouldn't say that. I mean that's just the point. It seems to me that we are inclined to say that chicha is disgusting. Period. Full stop.

TS: But not "They should stop drinking chicha."

SS: No. But that's a different question. Again, notice that you can pull those issues apart even in cases of morality. You shouldn't be nasty to your kindly maiden aunt, but I'm not going to stop you from doing that.

TS: But you don't even say "They shouldn't be drinking chicha."

SS: No, that's because the disgust system and the norm system are different. The disgust system isn't designed to affect your behavior toward other people in the way the norm system is.

TS: Let me take another example, a question from the list I sent you. One of the examples of moral disagreement in your work, something I focus on quite a bit in my own work as well, is on the existence of honor cultures—cultures that place great importance in responding aggressively to insults, especially insults to female chastity and the male's manhood. You discuss Nisbett's experiment, where letters are sent to employers in the South and the North in which the applicant reveals that he has been convicted for manslaughter after someone at a bar claimed to have slept with his fiancée. So here's my question: is it okay to beat the crap out of someone who insults you and your fiancée in South Carolina, but morally wrong to do that in Greenwich Village or Boulder, Colorado?

SS: It's just wrong. Period.

TS: It's just wrong. You're saying that because you're Steve Stich, brought up in New York. But if someone else who was brought up in the South says the opposite, that it's wrong to take that insult without a giving the guy a beat-down, they would equally justified. Both comments are equally justified.

SS: "Justified" is your terminology, not mine.

TS: Okay, right, so both comments are equally... equally what, then?

SS: Both comments are expressing deep facts about our internalized norms, which play an important role in determining who we are, or what kinds of people we are. We are very different kinds of people. But that's the end of it. If the question is, "Are my norms true, and theirs false?" the answer is *no*—norms aren't in that line of work.

TS: So the language is misleading. If the two of you are talking about the same thing, and one of you says "It's wrong" and the other says "It's not wrong," that sounds like a contradiction. But it's not.

SS: That's a traditional feature of any noncognitivist view.

TS: I guess in the same way that if you say chicha is disgusting and a Peruvian says it's not, you aren't contradicting each other, even though the language suggests that you are.

SS: Well, the linguistic issues are complex. It may well be that the appropriate account of the semantics of these sentences maintains that people are assuming a kind of objectivism; they both assume they are attributing an objective property to chicha. And if that's the case then they're both wrong.

TS: This is what's so interesting about the empirical work done on that question—on whether people do take morality to be objective. I guess there could be cross-cultural variation even there. It sounds like people in those cultures who don't require a justification for their actions, or even know what you're talking about, are a lot less objectivist in their moral thinking. I've always thought that Haidt's dumbfounding cases are evidence that people *do* believe they're appealing to something more objective when making moral judgments. Otherwise, why do they try so hard to keep justifying the judgments?

SS: Well, you may be right about that. But the part I would jump up and down on is your use of the word *people*.

TS: Sure, people may be different on this…

SS: Here's a hypothesis I've been thinking about lately. I don't know whether it's true, but I do plan to spend some time looking for relevant evidence. What the hypothesis claims is that the tradition of trying to justify normative claims in a deep and foundational way, the tradition of trying to provide something like philosophical or argumentative justifications for moral judgments—this is an *extremely* culturally local phenomenon. It's something that exists only in Western cultures and cultures that have been influenced by Western cultures. In many cultures, and for much of human history, providing that kind of justification has played no part in normative psychology.

TS: That's a fascinating hypothesis! I would love to learn more about that. And then it would be really interesting to learn why that tradition developed.[3]

SS: Yep, I think that's right; it certainly would be. It *might* be the case that the tradition is itself based on a culturally local norm (or a cluster of norms) governing the sorts of things one is allowed or required to say when a normative statement is challenged. That might explain your comment, a while back, when you said, "I don't see what *allows* you to say that." The hypothesis also has some rather provocative implications concerning work in moral psychology. If it's right, then the entire Kohlbergian tradition, which looks at the sorts of justifications that people offer for their moral judgments, may have been focused on a cultural artifact, rather than on universal features of moral development as Kohlberg thought.

TS: So Kohlberg was a great ethnographer, as someone once told Richard Nisbett...[4]

---

[3] In Chapter 5, Joe Henrich gives a hypothesis for why the tradition of moral justification might develop. He ties it to the existence of a legal system.

[4] Nisbett is a well-known psychologist at the University of Michigan. Once, when he was working on a theory that he believed applied universally to human cognition, a colleague told him that the theory was a great piece of ethnography. (In other words, his theory did a nice job describing features of contemporary Western culture.)

SS: Um, I'm not sure he was a great one, but yes, he was an ethnographer.

VI. SOME ILLUSIONS SHOULD
NOT BE CORRECTED.

TS: I think I might already have the answers to my last two questions. I was going to ask about the political implications of your view, how it might affect foreign policy decisions, things like that, but now I imagine you'll say that your view likely has no real implication along those lines.

SS: Right, exactly. It's far from clear to me that my view of the nature of the process underlying moral judgment has any substantive implications about what we should do. When I'm reflecting about what we should do when it comes to foreign policy or domestic policy, I'm being driven by a norm system that I've internalized. And, to be sure, there are lots of intriguing questions we could ask about the ways in which views about the psychology of the norm system might interact with the system itself; there are delicate dialectical issues here. But if the question is: whether my view has implications about the attitude we should have toward genital mutilation, or gay marriage, or feeding the starving in Darfur… as far as I can see, the answer is no.

TS: This is interesting: here's where you have a real disagreement with Josh Greene, whom I just interviewed. He has a polar-opposite view about the implications of learning about our moral psychology. He thinks that the more we understand about it, the more utilitarian we'll become. And he's an antirealist, but he thinks that utilitarianism is going to start making more sense to everyone after we learn what causes nonutilitarian judgments. I take it that you don't see any reason to think that would happen, or that it ought to happen?

SS: Ah, well, on the "ought to happen," I don't know; I'm not sure what that means. But on the "would happen," I think that's utterly laughable, absolutely laughable.[5] Think about the rough analogy with disgust. Many educated people realize that disgustingness is a property we project on to things. Does that in any way undermine the thought that someone barfing on your shirt is disgusting? No.

TS: So then I imagine you don't think your views on knowledge and morality have had much effect on your more day-to-day behavior, the way you make decisions, in your judgments about other people, fights with colleagues, perhaps...

SS: Well, my views have certainly led to fights with colleagues, but those are fights over the theories in question. But the answer to the question I think you really had in mind is no. The Müller-Lyer analogy is the right one. One can have theoretical views about how one's mind is working without those views having any significant effect on how the mind works.

TS: And we have no control over changing that? I don't know. Maybe here I'd agree with Josh Greene to some extent. Certainly, I've defended a view—I talked about this in my interview with Galen Strawson—which says that coming to the theoretical conclusion that our views on moral responsibility are untenable *can* have a practical effect on your day-to-day life. It can change the way we treat people and ourselves. Not, maybe, in the most dramatic cases, like when a family member is harmed, but in smaller instances. We become less resentful, less bitter. Less retributive perhaps. Gradually, over time.

SS: Is that a claim about what can happen? Is it a causal claim?

TS: Yes. I'm saying that views about moral responsibility can have that causal effect. I'm not claiming that there's decisive evidence to support that, but...

---

5 Greene's response: "Well, I'm writing a book defending my position on this."

SS: Well, taken in one way, what you said is certainly true. It is *possible* that views about moral responsibility could have that effect. But, to be a bit facetious, it is also *possible* that having belly-button lint could have that effect. But why should you think it *would*?

But let me give a more serious answer. In some of the work I've done with Chandra Sripada and Dan Kelly, we've explored what we call the "two sets of books hypothesis." It's an idea inspired, in part, by dual-processing theories that have been widely discussed in cognitive science in recent years. The basic idea is that moral judgments may be influenced by two very different sorts of psychological systems. One of these is what I've been calling the "norm system." It has many of the properties that dual-processing theorists attribute to "type-one" systems—it's fast, automatic, unconscious and cognitively impenetrable, and it has a longer evolutionary history. But in addition to the norm system, rules governing behavior may be stored in other components of the mind, components that have some of the properties usually associated with "type-two" systems. They are slower, evolutionarily newer, more cognitively penetrable, and some of the processing that takes place in them is accessible to consciousness. We know relatively little about the sorts of type-two systems that might store behavior governing rules; we don't understand how they succeed in generating motivation to comply with the rules they store. Now, if you are right that your views about moral responsibility (or other theoretical issues in moral psychology) have changed the way you treat people, I'd guess these changes are the product of type-two systems. A type-two system might also be involved in the culturally local tradition of providing justifications that we talked about earlier. There might be a rule embedded in a type-two system that said (roughly): If you can't come up with a justification for a certain sort of action, then you shouldn't do it.

TS: And that's another norm…

SS: Well, the terminology is potentially misleading here. I prefer to use the term *norm* for rules stored in the norm system. And indeed, the "If you can't justify it, don't do it" rule might be a culturally local norm. But if it's the sort of rule that you can be convinced of by philosophical argument or by psychological evidence, then it is probably in a cognitively penetrable type-two component of the mind, *not* in the norm system. And if that's the case, I would not call it a norm.

TS: One last thing about this perceptual-illusion analogy. When you call something an illusion, that means you know it's false, right? You know the lines aren't different lengths, even though they look that way. By analogy, you know that your views on, say, the practices of honor cultures aren't objectively correct, even though they appear that way. To the extent that you can design political institutions to deal with the reality behind moral judgments, rather than our illusions about them, then shouldn't we do that? In other words, to the extent that a given institution—perhaps our system of criminal justice—is based on the illusion of moral objectivity, shouldn't we design a system that corrects for this illusion?

SS: Well, first of all, let's be clear that this is a *moral* question, not a psychological question. And if I understand you correctly, it's a very general question. You're asking whether we should *always* design political institutions in a way that corrects for illusions. That's a question that I find hard to answer because, in many cases, I just don't know what it would be to design or redesign political institutions in a way that "corrects" for psychological illusions. Earlier in our conversation, you seemed to be suggesting that if moral objectivity is an illusion and people became aware of that fact, they might no longer condemn practices like genital mutilation, which accord with the norms of other cultures. Would legalizing genital mutilation be a way of "correcting" for the illusion of objectivity? I don't know, since you haven't explained what "correcting" means. But if the answer is *yes*—if legalizing genital mutilation would be a way of correcting for the illusion—then my answer to your question is a resounding *no*! We most definitely should *not* always design legal systems in a way that corrects for illusions. ✶

9

WILLIAM IAN MILLER

CODES OF HONOR

"Honor above all, Dog. Honor ain't cost-effective, but y'all must do yo' utmost 2 preserve it, cuz in tha end, it have tha most value."

—Herbert Kornfeld

One of the most inspired creations of the parody newspaper the *Onion* is Herbert Kornfeld, columnist and accounts-receivable supervisor at a regional office-supply company. The joke of the column—which ran for eight years and somehow never got old—is that this impossibly nerdy-looking Jewish accountant talks and acts like a gangsta rapper and all-around badass. Kornfeld's obsession with honor is modeled on what sociologists often call the "honor culture" of inner-city gang life. The term refers to societies or groups that place tremendous importance on acquiring honor and status, and on avenging slights, insults, and offenses. (Kornfeld zealously defends "tha Accountz Reeceevable code," and is quick to whip out his "letta opener of death" at even the mildest hint of disrespect.)[1]

Over the past fifty or so years, researchers from a wide range of disciplines have observed and studied cultures with honor-based values systems. They span across history (Homeric Greece, medieval Iceland) and exist today all over the world. Their values can be found in smaller communities within a larger society (the Mafia, pockets of the American South), or they can run through an entire country.[2] Many Arab and Islamic societies are thought to be honor cultures, and as a result research on this topic has attracted the attention of political and military strategists. Former US Army Major William McCallister, for example, has attributed the US's initial unpopularity with Iraqis during the Iraq war to, in part, our failure to grasp the pervasive role that the concepts of shame and honor play in Iraqi society; they are as important to the Iraqis as land and water. McCallister, who now consults with the Marines in Iraq, writes that "It has taken us four years to realize that we must execute operations within the existing cultural frame of reference."[3]

When honor cultures are discussed in intellectual or academic circles, however, there is often an implicit assumption that their values, especially their preoccupation with revenge, are primitive, backward, irrational—of scholarly interest certainly, but something we in the civilized West are grateful to have moved beyond. Not William Ian Miller. Miller, a professor of law at the University of Michigan, has spent much of his career writing about the honor cultures of tenth- and eleventh-century Iceland as they are described in the

---

[1] Tragically, on April 30, 2007, Herbert Kornfeld was found dead in his company's copy room, a victim of "white-on-white" violence and the ongoing office-worker turf wars.

[2] Of course, the differences between honor cultures and nonhonor cultures are a matter of degree, not kind. Values and attitudes related to honor can be found in all societies, but they are emphasized more in those that are classified as honor cultures. As you'll see below, Miller believes that the differences between honor and nonhonor cultures are not as stark as some scholars believe.

[3] See *smallwarsjournal.com/blog/2007/07/coin-in-a-tribal-society-1*.

amazing Icelandic sagas (written one hundred to three hundred years later). He's one of the world's leading authorities on honor cultures, and also one of their greatest advocates. Far from condescending to these cultures, Miller sings their praises.[4] He holds up the lives of his saga Icelanders as a model, something to respect, admire, even emulate. Miller belongs to a small but growing number of legal theorists who believe that the distinction between justice and revenge is artificial, a fabrication of philosophers. According to Miller, the concept of justice has its foundation in revenge, in getting even— and if you're looking for subtle and complex analyses of revenge, the Icelandic sagas are second to none.

William Ian Miller has published numerous scholarly articles and eight books, including *Bloodtaking and Peacemaking, Humiliation,* and *Eye for an Eye.* His books are scholarly, entertaining, and highly personal, an almost-unheard-of combination in academic writing. I met Miller at the Grizzly Peak Brewing Company in Ann Arbor. For better or worse, we conducted the interview over, well, several beers. Our discussion (only a portion of which can be reproduced here) spanned more than three hours and a wide range of topics, including Miller's experience growing up Jewish in Green Bay, Wisconsin, my near-fight with my landlord, the appalling hypocrisy of the Israeli University boycott, great revenge movies, and, of course, Miller's views on honor cultures in Medieval Iceland and elsewhere.

November 2008

I. WHAT IS AN HONOR CULTURE?

TAMLER SOMMERS: At the risk of overgeneralizing things a bit, what characterizes an honor or honor-based culture?

WILLIAM IAN MILLER: It's not an easy question, actually. One

---

[4] Miller noted in an email that this is in large part a rhetorical strategy, "designed to shock the complacent view that honor cultures are primitive and not something each and every one of us is familiar with at some level."

characteristic—and this is why you can have honor cultures within a larger culture—is that there's a roughly egalitarian grouping, where people are very anxious about where they stand, relative to each other. And for them, honor makes a big difference because that's how they determine relative ranking.

TS: Why is that so important to them?

WIM: Well, I don't want to make claims about "hardwiring," but we'd always much rather be looked up to than looked down upon. It's very hard to imagine a culture where being looked down upon is a virtue. And, of course, if you make it a virtue, then it becomes that which is honored. So Christianity has this thing—some Hindu cultures, too—where status was conferred by how wretched you could be. Then it just became inverse honor: "Hey, I'm more wretched than you are." Yeah, I can show I'm more wretched, I can fast twenty years longer than you can. I can sit on a flag pole for six months with no clothes on. You could only do that for three months. So no matter what, it's about status and competitiveness.

TS: Aside from sitting naked on flagpoles, what are some typical ways to gain status in honor cultures?

WIM: You know, there's not a set of rules. There're certain people who get the benefit of the doubt. And they get the benefit of the doubt maybe because their ancestors were honorable. What's interesting to me in studying honor cultures is how redeemable *dishonor* is. Honor is never tested if you're not already down; if you don't get knocked down and see if you can reassert it. So some kind of dissing is built into the system, where you've got to experience being up against the wall. Where you're tested.

TS: What are some of the tests?

WIM: There're a bunch of tests. The prime virtue is clearly courage. So test number one kind of resembles playing chicken.

You have to show that you don't scare easy. Everybody knows that people are scared, but you have to show that it's not going to interfere with your actions. So keeping a level head under stress— you know, not everyone can be a physical tough guy. And the sagas are so good about this. They show a lot of physical weenies who are dominating. It's because they're smart. And they don't scare easy. That's the one thing you've gotta have—not scaring easy. You've got to keep your cool.

But suppose you've got a lot of courage, you don't scare easy, and then you have one bad day. You run away from battle one time, or you break down and cry. Soldiers tend to be more forgiving about this—they know everyone has their good days and bad days. But in honor cultures? If you have a bad day, that can always be brought up to ridicule you. That might well be commemorated in song. Even though you can redeem it to some extent, it's still there to…create tension in situations such as feasts. Someone will get up and say, "Everyone thinks you're so brave, but that's not what they said about you at the battle of so-and-so." And then the question is: can you take that kind of "dis"? Are you cool enough to be able to just laugh at it? Or does that guy have to be taken out and whacked?

TS: And you believe that these kinds of attitudes rise out of situations where everyone is roughly on equal ground?

WIM: I'd put it like this. Honor cultures are a necessary condition of roughly egalitarian communities. Because people will compete for precedence that isn't articulated, it's always how you're standing in the jealous eyes of fellow competitors.

TS: You were talking before about being in grade school, where people start out fairly equal. I guess there's quite a bit of honor-culture stuff that goes on in school.

WIM: Right. You know, I remember growing up that the test for little boys would be to not cry. And you would keep pushing yourself. And all you got if you survived this day's test, jumping off a ledge or something, whatever the contest, was to show you weren't a chicken. It didn't prove that you were honorable, it just proved you weren't a coward for the day.

TS: Are there any other attitudes or practices that, broadly speaking, most honor cultures share?

WIM: Not wanting to be laughed at, unless you're purposely playing the clown, in which case *not* being laughed at would be a dis. But not wanting to be the object of derisive laughter shows how much honor is still alive and well, even among types like us: suppose you slip on the ice and take a bad spill. What's the first thing you care about? Whether you were seen, right? Not how much your back is hurting. You'll deal with that later.

TS: Many people hear about these honor-based attitudes and values and they dismiss them as violent, primitive, irrational. Why is that?

WIM: That's because the people who say those kinds of things tend to be academics and clergy—who got beaten up on the playground. And that's kind of dismissive, but it's partly true. Because if they felt they were *winning* at this game... I mean, where do *they* think virtue lies? In reason, argumentation, disputation! The very things they're good at! Now come on—give me a break! Look, reason's just fine. But these old thuggish warriors that I study, when reason came in, they saw it as a tool of clerics to get land from them. And they weren't wrong! There's a politics of reason, right? You know that's true.

TS: Sure, but...

WIM: But that's just one answer. Why do honor cultures get dissed? Because the people who are dissing it don't win at it. Kind of a trivial answer. It's Nietzsche's answer. The other answer is—

well, I'm not sure *I* want to live in my saga world, I'm not sure I have the nerves to do it. I respect them, I admire them. I think they're *nobler* than we are at some level. I mean, why is it that these guys make stories we still thrill to, whereas us academics, our virtues make for the tediousness of faculty meetings? You gotta say that there's a falling off!

TS: At the same time, it's not all fun and excitement. There's some grisly stuff that goes on too, right?

WIM: But it's not necessarily honor that makes honor cultures get a bad name. It's the substantive issues on which honor is fought out.

TS: The aggression, the violence, the attitudes towards women…

WIM: Yeah, okay, but what about an honor culture like my saga Iceland guys, who couldn't give a damn about whether their women screwed around? They didn't care. But now take an Islamic one, where you gotta kill the woman [if she screws around[. We think, That's horrible, the honor culture! But it has nothing to do with honor culture. What it has to do with is that the underlying norms about which they decide that honor are at stake.

TS: You say something along those lines in your book *Humiliation*. That in Islamic societies, and in certain Mediterranean cultures, too, honor is linked with shame—and they link shame with women.

WIM: Well, it's linked so tightly with chastity. In the [Icelandic] Northlands they could care less about it. That's an exaggeration, but they put very little store by virginity in comparison with Mediterranean cultures—whether Christian, Muslim, or Jewish.

TS: Which made me think about guys calling each other pussies all the time.

WIM: Yeah, we still do it. In my courage book [*The Mystery of Courage*], I talk about people saying: "He's one tough mother." That doesn't mean—you don't connect toughness with being a woman. It means he's one tough motherfucker. And then, right, "What a pussy," meaning coward. Of course, this gender stuff was alive and well in the Northlands. It's just that it didn't get actualized into caring what their women did. But the language, the insults, were the same.

TS: What do you think accounts for this difference in caring about chastity? Is it a religion thing?

WIM: No, I don't know why. We don't know what the cause and effect was. Was it because the saga people weren't obsessed with virginity that women had more power, or was it because they had more power and that they could demand more sexual freedom?

TS: You say in *Eye for an Eye* that some honor cultures are "well-functioning" and some aren't. And that in some radical Islamic and inner-city gang settings, things aren't well-functioning. Can you say more about that?

WIM: This gets more complicated than I can manage in a few words, but let me try. What the inner city is missing is older people with property and power to force violent young men to keep their violence within limits. Now the older generations have nothing to threaten the hot-headed with to keep their violence within bounds. Honor cultures, like any well-functioning culture, have to *keep violence down* to levels people can live with, with *live*, I guess, taking on a literal edge. In a certain kind of Islamic setting, at least the one we fear in the West, it's the old men who have seemed a little too willing to let their young die, while they keep themselves out of harm's way. A culture of martyrdom can get out of hand—as it did among early Christians and Jews in the first century, and medieval centuries, and Islam now. Christianity tried to resolve it by rejecting volunteering for martyrdom. You had to wait until it came to you.

II. WHY ARE HONOR
CULTURES SO SMART?

TS: At the end of *Eye for an Eye,* you write that it's obvious to you that people in these cultures are better psychologists and social psychologists than we are today, and that we're not as smart now as we were when we worried more about honor than pleasure. Can you elaborate on that?

WIM: I think a subpolemic in all my academic work—all my writing, even the monograph on the Icelandic sagas—is awe and respect for these people, for how smart they are. And why are they so smart? Because they're better than we are at discerning motive in others. And why is that? Because the stakes are so damn high. They get it wrong, they're dead.

TS: Or they're dishonored. Which is just as bad in some cases.

WIM: Right. So it makes them hyperaware of others. I mean, you want fellow-feeling? They have it a hundred times more than our sentimentalized culture of "Oh, I feel your pain." I see a big downturn in smartness about discerning motive, intention, inner states, with the rise of depth psychology. Freud, Lacan—a joke compared to the British moralists of the eighteenth century, a joke compared to my blood feuders, my Icelandic saga writers. A joke compared to Thucydides.

TS: Do you think we deceive ourselves as to what our motives are?

WIM: No, not really. Self-deception is alive and well in all cultures. It's necessary to get from one day to the next. Although we openly promote self-deception now in a way that they never did. The self-esteem movement, stuff like that. But back then, you had to really care more about what others thought about you. I'm not sure that's always a good thing. It can be crippling in some ways.

TS: Would you say that they're pursuing honor, but at least they're open about it? They know they're pursuing honor. We pursue honor. But we tell ourselves we're pursuing something else. I don't know, well-being, intellectual achievement…

WIM: Right—intellectual achievement for its own sake. Or everyone's number one in their own way. So we're a whole society of number ones. What a joke! I mean Nietzsche is right at some point about this. We're a culture of *ressentiment*. We've constructed a world so that a loser can claim they're the winner. But Nietzsche doesn't get it exactly right either. Because at one level, he's whining nonstop about why *his* guys didn't win.

TS: Didn't win?

WIM: They got outsmarted by the Jews! You lost—stop whining about it. Your blond beast got outsmarted by the Jews—who unfortunately got too smart for their own good by developing Christianity, which really screwed the Jews but good.

TS: Yeah, we're still reeling from that… But to get back to how smart honor cultures are…

WIM: There's so much depth and subtlety. For example, the honor systems I'm familiar with didn't want anyone getting too good, because then they became your lord, and it wasn't a roughly egalitarian community any longer. So what you wanted to do—if you were in the running for first, in order to live, to avoid getting gunned down as the fastest gun in the West—was to care about other's people's envy and not make it hurt them too much. You had to cultivate an attitude that didn't make people *feel* your dominance too much. Or else they would gang together and take you out. So there were these built-in leveling mechanisms. Because people were envying you, and envy is a dangerous sentiment. At the same time, envy was the only sign that you'd made it. So you wanted to be envied. But you didn't want their envy to be too painful or they'd take you out.

TS: How do you strike the balance?

WIM: Well, the cultures differ on this. Certain cultures are like the rap style—"I'm the best, no one can touch me"—and even the Icelanders are like this. There's a certain cultivation of poetry, of song, that tells everyone you're so good. At the same time, that's usually delimited to very ritualized domains where everyone knows it's fun that this rhyming self-promotion is going on. Outside of that, you don't want to make people feel the pain of your dominance. You want to cultivate a style of false modesty, graciousness, generosity. Which still is a sign that you're up there. There's a certain style of false modesty where everyone knows it's false. But if you didn't do it, they would hate your guts.

TS: If you rubbed it in their face…

WIM: Yeah, so you want to be very chary of other people's envy, but you want to know that it's there.

III. ACADEMIC WEENIES

TS: You often talk about how these values and attitudes can be found, sometimes disguised, in environments that we don't associate with honor cultures—academia, for example.

WIM: The difference between honor cultures, like my saga guys, the *Iliad*, and academic culture now, is that the academic weenies will pretend that they are nonviolent and don't believe in any of this "male" type of assertion, when of course they're fighting over who gets what office, who gets what lectureship, who didn't, and the same pecking order stuff takes place. We're in denial!

TS: In denial of what?

WIM: In denial of just how much envy and relative standing drives our world. You see people fighting over the silliest forms of precedence that have been the subject of moralist derision from time immemorial. Seating arrangements. My uncle at my sister's wedding stopped speaking to my mother, not his blood relative, because he wasn't seated close enough to the bride's table.

TS: Isn't there a saga you talk about where something like that happens?

WIM: Yes. Somebody's got the seat of honor. They rank the seats. One guy puts his fist next to the guy in the seat of honor. He says, "Gudmund, what do you think of this fist?" "That's a big fist." "Do you think it could do much damage?" "Sure." "How much damage?" "It could probably break some bones." "Do you think it could break your bones?" "Sure," he says. "How would such broken bones appeal to you, Gudmund?" "Not at all." " Then get out of my seat." Gudmund exchanged seats with the guy.

TS: So there's a hierarchy everywhere, it's just a matter of degree.

WIM: To what degree it's official and demarcated by badges or medals or formal noble ranking is in one kind of hierarchy. It's different when the hiearachy is unofficial, when it becomes a matter of these little signs—how I look at you when I talk to you, say, or who gets listened to and who doesn't. Those are the little indicators of where people stand.

TS: But what about the violence in honor cultures? That at least seems to be more under wraps in everyday situations in other kinds of societies.

WIM: Here's the thing about that. I wrote about this in *Humiliation*, a chapter on violence. My high school was this working-class high school, it was pretty rough and tumble, at least to my fearful mind. But I was only in two or three fights my whole time in junior high and high school. Nevertheless, my whole life was geared around being in a fight. So if you actually measured the amount of violence that went on in my life, there wasn't that much. But the threat of it was always there, and it governed a whole lot about who you wanted to be friends with, who you dealt with in a certain way. You're always trying to either not offend or to show that you were not afraid in this or that setting. But if you added up the amount of actual violence, there wasn't that much. But it still was the dominating principle in everyone's behavior, to make sure it didn't happen to them, or if it happened to them, to make sure it happened on their terms. But then I became an academic, so this could just be the coward's-eye view.

TS: In the end of *Humiliation*, you say that you want the reader, most likely an educated non-honor-embracing reader, to come away with the psychological complexity, the danger, involving our everyday encounters.

WIM: Like this encounter right now…

IV. "MILLER THINKS HE'S THE NORM. AND HE'S NUTS!"

TS: So let me ask you this, because I worry about it myself. I've done some work on honor cultures recently, and like you say, it gives you sort of a new prism, a new way of viewing day-to-day encounters. But often when I'm going on about these things, my wife will accuse me of artificially bringing my work into these situations, projecting it on real life. I remember Galen Strawson, in a review of *Humiliation*, accused you of something similar: generalizing from your own experience. And, like you told me earlier, you grew up as one of a few Jewish kids in Green Bay—you grew up in an honor culture, having to fight for respect. But maybe it's not like that for everyone—people with different backgrounds which made their childhood less of a fight, less competitive. Do you worry that you're doing that at least a little bit—projecting your own experience on the rest of the world?

WIM: You know, people accuse of me of this. I have a couple of colleagues who joke, you know, "Miller thinks he's *l'homme moyen sensual,* that he's the norm. And he's nuts!" And of course I think, "No, you're an academic weenie, you just haven't grown up normal." Anyone who's grown up normal knows what I'm talking about.

TS: Okay, but, you know, even from our conversation, when you said that even our encounter right now is fraught with psychological complexity, honor—I don't know, I might be deluded, but it doesn't feel that way to me.

WIM: No, we're not trying to one-up each other or anything like that. It's more defensive. Neither of us wants to think that the other one is a fraud or an idiot, right? And we would be sick to death if we thought that that was the sense we gave. We'd lie awake at night, wondering if he thought I'm a total idiot.

TS: I guess I see that...[5]

WIM: I'm always lying awake at night. I'm an insomniac. I'm always thinking: did I get dissed? I didn't think so at the time but... I'm always thinking about these things to get revenge for. And my students will ask me—they can see I'm hot-tempered: "Professor Miller, did you get drawn to the sagas because you were like that, or did you become the way you are because of the sagas?" I say, That's a good question. I ask that of myself, and I think maybe it's both. I was drawn to them because they spoke to me. At the same time, they set a standard for me to live up to. Talk about getting totally involved in your research.

TS: Another person working on honor cultures at Michigan, Richard Nisbett, defended the idea that certain values and attitudes might be better suited for certain kinds of environments. So

---

[5] My wife, when reading this, looked up at me and said, "You *guess* you see that? You're exactly like that!"

attitudes focusing on defending honor are better suited for scarce environments, lawless environments.

WIM: Material scarcity, yes.

TS: Also lawlessness.

WIM: Material scarcity, mostly. Material scarcity is what raises the stakes. If you're in a rich culture, you can afford to have someone break into your house.

TS: Right, it's annoying, but—

WIM: But we're not going to be destroyed. Whereas if somebody steals their lamb, it might mean their kid dies. The loss of the lamb reduces the amount of calories available for consumption and so they might well lose a member of the family. So the high hatred, the killing of the thief in those kinds of cultures, it's not that the thief is stealing a marginal dollar from a millionaire, he's close to committing attempted murder, or even murder.

TS: So in that kind of culture, material scarcity, where a single act of theft could cost you your family, it's probably good to cultivate a kind of reputation.

WIM: A reputation of "don't tread on me." I actually think those cultures when they're working right are more defensive than offensive. And they want to control the jerk who's going around picking fights. But they also have to show "don't mess with me." But how do show "don't mess with me" without being a little belligerent yourself?

But back to the Strawson thing, where he thinks I'm imposing my own experience on the world. I get accused of this all the time—especially when I give a talk to a group with a high number of academic feminists. As soon as I start talking about girls and high school, you can see that they know what I'm talk-

ing about, but they'll be resisting. And I'll answer them by saying something like, I have to work hard—I have to work *really*
hard to imagine a world where I don't feel that I have to settle
a score, or in which I don't care where I stand. I can't imagine
what that kind of world would be like, a world of either complete refusal to recognize a wrong, or a harm done to you, or one
in which, when you do have a harm done to you, your first impulse is to forgive. But you don't have to take a leap of faith to
imagine my world. You've been fighting against it your whole
life! You've been openly at war with it. In fact, forgiveness is often its own form of revenge.

TS: But don't you think there's a spectrum, some variation in tem-
perament? This connects to the environmental issue, since different
environments can dictate different kinds of attitudes, right? You
might be at one extreme, at least in academia, and other people
might truly be less interested in status or avenging slights. Maybe
they don't care. Why would it have to be so uniform?

WIM: It wouldn't have to be uniform, and some people don't care,
yes. And you know, there's the same spectrum in honor cultures;
some people care too much. And people don't like them. They're
the types that create too much violence. But it's crazy to think that
these kinds of attitudes aren't prevalent or that we can repress them
entirely.

TS: Sure. And I'm not denigrating them, or calling them primitive.
I'm the same way—I'm a hothead. It's the Israeli in me. And I also
love rap music, I joke about it with my friends, I joke about it with
my students. But it's gotta be a joke, right? I've got to be making
fun of myself while I'm admiring…

WIM: Yeah, of course. The idea of me, a scrawny sixty-two-year-
old academic playing tough guy with my students… it's, well, it's a
joke. So I'm constantly self-mocking.

TS: It has to be a joke, or else *we'd* be the joke.

WIM: Exactly. I actually do worry that I am overly romanticizing these guys, as part of an active and silly fantasy life I've been cursed with since grade school.

TS: I thought of this because in your books—it's actually very funny—you make a lot of self-deprecating references, calling yourself an academic weakling, things like that. I do the same thing in my classes. But underneath that—I genuinely wish I was a little tougher, a little harder. I mean, I don't wish I was dealing crack on the corners of East Baltimore, but at the same time…

WIM: Somewhere I talked about this commercial "Be Like Mike." The commercial was so smart because you don't want to lose the consciousness of you. You want to be *you,* but with Michael Jordan's skills. I want to be *me,* but also as tough as some of these guys I study. But of course, if I were that, then it wouldn't be me.

TS: Here's one thing I was thinking about. It's ridiculous to think that I could be some badass, like Wee-Bey on *The Wire.* And if I tried, I'd be the laughingstock of the world. I'm kind of a laughing-stock anyway; whenever I say I like hip-hop, everyone calls me the guy from *Office Space.* But think of the flip side of this. In the West, we want to take people from the other side and convert them to nonhonor culture values. This happens in the inner city, with schools, and to some extent in Iraq, right? So here's my question: Wouldn't it be just as humiliating, just as incongruous, for some people steeped in honor-culture attitudes and values, to try to take on values like humility, shrugging off insults, turn the other cheek stuff? Wouldn't it seem just as ridiculous for them, in their own eyes and in others', as for me to try to be a badass?

WIM: Well, look. Jewish kids and Asian kids. Part of the competition was how smart you were. But that wasn't the whole Jewish story. The Lower East Side of New York… You know, if you look at the 1920s Green Bay Packers photos, more than a few of the linemen on the team were Jewish.

TS: Really?

WIM: Yeah. The immigrants are the tough guys.

TS: What happened to us?

WIM: Yeah, right, what happened to us? My daughter told me a wonderful story about Bugsy Siegel. Some Haganah guys come to him to ask him for money. And Bugsy, he don't know from nothing about the Haganah. So they explain to him who they are, we need guns, we need weapons. He says "What, you mean Jews are killing people?" They say "Yeah, we need to, we're fighting." He says, "Jews are killing people?" And he writes them a check.

TS: That's very funny, I love that. But it doesn't exactly answer my question. Let me put it like this: you see in reports from Iraq that some officers come back almost bewildered by the honor codes. One former army guy said that honor and shame are their moral currency, and that until we understand that, we're screwed. Do you think a general misunderstanding of honor cultures has led to (honest, in a way) mistakes, like thinking we'll be greeted as liberators, or that we can establish a democracy without too much pain and loss of life?

WIM: It isn't honor culture the officers don't understand; hell, they live in one. It's the particular substantive matters that trigger honor concerns in Iraq—just what precisely they will take as a big offense and what they'll shrug off. That's where the misunderstandings take place.

V. THE SINS OF THE FATHER

TS: I want to talk about the connection between honor and revenge on the one hand and justice on the other. Many see the two as miles apart, right? First of all, in America we think justice should be blind, administered by an unbiased third party. Juries who have no personal stake whatsoever in the offense. But in honor cultures, justice is very personal. And they think it ought to be personal.

WIM: Well, it is and it isn't. In honor cultures, you consult. Because it's not clear that you're the only wronged person. There's usually a group of people who are wronged; they have to sit down and make a decision. These are usually small communities in which this happens. And you consult with your neighbors to see what will be tolerated because you don't want to offend them. And so, in fact, there's more of a communal decision-making process than the antirevenge ideology wants to admit. The antirevenge ideology wants to make revenge a matter of your own rage, but I just have too many sources where people are told, sorry, no, you can't take revenge. It's not politically feasible. They weigh a lot of things that a legal system of justice would weigh, and they weigh even more, like the state of prior relations.

TS: Sort of like going to a Mafia boss, and the boss lets them know how far they can go.

WIM: Yeah, yeah—there's discussion. And in my sources, if someone goes off and takes revenge without consulting his kinsmen, they hang him out to dry. Because, look. If you can die for your uncle or brother's behavior, you have an absolute right to demand that before they go and kill they consult you first.

TS: This was the second difference I was going to bring up. In our tradition—our conception of justice—you're only responsible for what you yourself do. You're not responsible for the actions of your uncle or cousin.

WIM: You see that even in our revenge-genre movies. We isolate the avenger, we give him no kin. He's not responsible to any-

one but his own inner lights. It's American Protestantism trium-
phant. And that's not what any revenge culture looks like. Because
when you go out and take revenge, you're hanging out your kids,
you're hanging out your brothers, cousins, and they demand a say.
Of course, sometimes they'll also demand that you *take* revenge.

TS: And you're obligated to take revenge sometimes on their be-
half, to avenge an insult to them, right? But this seems like a real
difference, too. We certainly have a view of justice where people
can't be blamed or punished for something they didn't bring about,
either through intention or negligence. But honor cultures will re-
taliate against people who didn't even commit the offense, brothers
or relatives of offenders, and that seems perfectly appropriate to
them. They don't see anything wrong with that.

WIM: No, they don't. It's totally fine.

TS: You talk about one case in a saga, where a man took revenge
against the brother of someone who hurt him years ago. And the
brother hadn't even been in the country at the time of the original offense!

WIM: Right, that's right—he wasn't in the country. See, there's a
bunch of ways these guys conceptualize revenge. One is that it's a
juridical act, getting even for past offenses. The other is forward-
looking. They're the best of utilitarians. In revenge cultures, it's my
turn—your turn, right? So if I kill a guy's brother, I gotta deal with
him, the *guy.* So why don't I start with *him,* if it makes better practical sense to get him now, say because I would rather not take my
turn on defense with him playing offense; so I take him out ahead
of time, for his brother who wronged me who may in fact be not
as frightening. So they're looking ahead to who they're going to
play defense against.

TS: I wonder if there's also a different way of seeing blameworthi-
ness here, the conditions for being truly blameworthy.

WIM: What do you mean by "truly blameworthy"?

TS: To deserve blame, to get what's really coming to you.

WIM: You know, one of the things that drives me crazy about our modern culture is that we medicalize so much, so that you can't hold somebody culpable because they have some syndrome, some disorder. That doesn't stop us from blaming someone for having the syndrome or the disorder. It just postpones the question. Let's say there's an unlucky person, a *schlemiel*. One time being a schlemiel, okay. Two times being a schlemiel, ehh. Three times, we start blaming the guy. We call him a schlemiel. Which means he's culpable, he's a schlemiel!

TS: But we still have this distinction of what you are, and what you're responsible for being.

WIM: We try to trick ourselves, maybe, into the obviousness of that distinction, but…

TS: Okay, we trick ourselves. There's still a difference, right? Because some of these honor cultures, they don't trick themselves. There's no pretense that you're not responsible for things that don't trace back to something you did, something that you did intentionally.

WIM: Well, that depends. Here you have to look culture by culture.

TS: Take honor killings. Aside from the horrible barbarism of the whole practice, one thing that baffles people in America is that a killing can happen even when the woman was raped. She was raped, she had no intention of having sex, no control over the act, but she's still culpable, she still has to die.

WIM: You end up telling a "they had it coming" story to yourself, perhaps, or maybe it is that being unlucky is itself an offense. Insurance companies think so. They charge you for your bad luck, say if you're accident-prone though never at fault in any particular accident, just always in the wrong place at the wrong time.

TS: You can also tell a story by projecting some kind of weird intention on her—the way she dressed...

WIM: Or where she was at the time, right...

TS: Yeah. Or you could think that intention doesn't matter that much. It happened, she's responsible. Period. That seems weird coming from the perspective of people who place so much stock in what we *meant* to do when determining responsibility. But maybe there's a lot of variation in how much intention matters for culpability.

WIM: Here's the thing. It is psychologically and culturally variable when and how we decide to fix what somebody's intention was. We look at a whole range of things, including how happy they were made by the harm they caused you. Did they benefit by it? Fixing intention is a complicated thing. The person isn't a good judge of his own intentions. And third parties can be bad judges, though not subject to the same biases. So we have to make some social judgment as to how to judge intention and when that judgment should be made.

TS: That's definitely one possible explanation for, say, how honor killings are seen from inside. That intention is fixed in some different way. All I'm trying to suggest as another possible explanation is that we're projecting our own obsession with intention on people who simply aren't as concerned about whether people intended to do something or not when deciding about culpability.

WIM: That's right, I think. But they can't afford to have intention matter that much. At the same time, you'll see discussions in the sagas, where they regret having to kill someone—it's too bad, he's a nice guy, whatever—but they'll get the most honor if they hit him.

So there are discussions of culpability, but it can be trumped. They have these other issues. Actually, I think we can focus so much on intention and culpability because we have elaborate systems of insurance. They didn't. So in some respects, what appears to us as their lack of concern with intention is really a very deep concern that they be compensated for any harm you or yours bore some kind of causal connection to. Hell, if you didn't mean it. My son is dead and I have lost his support and fighting capability, to say nothing of my honor, if I let him lie uncompensated for.

TS: True, but I still wonder if it's a different view of culpability. Take something like original sin. It's always struck me as bizarre that Adam ate the apple, or Eve ate the apple, and somehow I'm guilty, it's my fault. What did I have to do with it? That was their business! And theologian philosophers will bend over backwards to impute some weird intention on us—we *would* have eaten the apple, or Adam is human nature, and we're human, whatever. But part of me thinks: whoever came up with that story, they didn't care. You didn't eat the apple, too bad! You're still responsible. You're still guilty.

WIM: Whoever thought the sins of the father weren't passed on to the son...?

TS: Germans today feeling responsible for what their ancestors did. They weren't alive during the Holocaust, but my Dad certainly still wants to blame them.

WIM: And Jews, c'mon. We're blamed for everything.

TS: Right, even stuff we didn't do.

WIM: Even things our ancestors didn't do. What nobody did!

TS: So I wonder if we're the weird ones to focus so much on our intentions. And this reaches its apex in the free-will debate, where the conditions for responsibility can sometimes be impossible—

you have to self-create, create yourself out of nothing.

WIM: Yeah, I think the ancient cultures got this much better. They don't deny free will, it's just that they're not obsessive about it. They think you can blame people for being sick, for crossing the street at the wrong time. And in fact, in a folk way, we do this all the time. It's just not official. But you know, in the saga book, I actually say the opposite—that they do care about these things— that they're not as *other* as we make them out to be. That's because there are all these discussions about having to whack a guy even though he didn't deserve it. They're aware of the tragedy of these things. They're hyperaware of the tragic side of their way of set- tling matters. It's not arbitrary, they're not doing this out of lack of self-reflection.

VI. "ALL REVENGE IS COMEDY. IT'S A HAPPY ENDING."

TS: You've written a lot about the role of honor and revenge in movies. Is there a movie you think best gets across some of what we're talking about?

WIM: I actually tell my class that if you want to look at maybe the best revenge movie ever made, it might be *The Princess Bride*. Inigo Montoya can bring tears to anyone's eyes. I mean, here you are in the midst of a comedy—a generic shtick Jewish comedy—and the revenge theme comes on, and all of a sudden it becomes powerful, moving, tears. Not tears of sentimentality, but tears because there's some great truth here. You're at the core of the moral universe. It's so brilliant, and this isn't in the book version of *The Princess Bride,* just in the movie—where Inigo says at the end—he's killed the guy, and he says, "Now what the hell do I do? I've been in the re- venge business so long, I don't know what to do." His whole being has been consumed with revenge. Auden has a very smart essay where he talks about Hamlet, and how if he were to take revenge, his whole being would be extinguished in the process.

TS: My four-year-old daughter knows the speech by heart (Montoya's, not Hamlet's). "Hello. My name is Inigo Montoya. You killed my father. Prepare to die."

WIM: It's one of the greatest acting jobs ever. It's wonderful. Maybe the best revenge movie of all time. And it's a comedy. This isn't my idea; some Greek scholar said this. All revenge is comedy. It's a happy ending. It might be a feud that never ends. So then it's a bunch of happy endings.

TS: But what about a movie like *Unforgiven,* which you've written about, too. On the one hand, it's a happy ending, it's satisfying. But…

WIM: Can you imagine *Unforgiven* ending with Eastwood saying, "Okay, it's forgiven? Ah, Little Bill, it's okay, I know you didn't mean it. Ned just died on you, I'll let it go."

TS: Not as satisfying, yeah. Any other good revenge movies?

WIM: Name a movie you really like, and I bet 80 percent of them will have revenge lurking somewhere, giving it its edge. Take perhaps one of the greatest movies of all time: *Sunset Blvd.* Revenge? Sure, Wilder's on Hollywood, Norma's on Hollywood, and on talking itself. Maybe I'm stretching it a bit. Being a Clint Eastwood fan, I love his earliest self-directed western, *High Plains Drifter.* But Clint's revenge movies violate the rules of Icelandic feuding practice. In that movie he overdoes it; he vastly exceeds his just warrant for revenge. In Iceland, say fifty people attack your brother and kill him. You can't kill fifty or even twenty of them in revenge, though all are legally culpable. Anyway, in revenge, as in love, there are no easy answers. It's complex stuff with the local details, and the littlest shadings and nuances matter greatly.

Let's have another beer. ★

ACKNOWLEDGMENTS

Although I didn't know it at the time, this project was launched in late 2002 when Vendela Vida offered me the chance to interview a philosopher of my choice for the inaugural issue of the *Believer*. I was in graduate school at Duke University planning a dissertation on free will, and thought immediately of Galen Strawson, a celebrity in the field. Over the years, Vendela continued to allow me the freedom to select researchers whose work I found fascinating and relevant to my own pursuits. I owe a deep debt of gratitude to her for providing me with these opportunities and for being such an effective and savvy editor. Thanks also to Eli Horowitz for his help in tying the book together conceptually and thematically, and to all the people at the *Believer* and *McSweeney's* for making this project possible.

Grants from the Research Enhancement Fund at the University of Minnesota, Morris, and the Small Grants Program at the University of Houston provided funding for some of the travel for the interviews. I am grateful to my colleagues at both institutions and also at Duke University for their enthusiastic support of what some might consider a nonacademic project. Thanks to Christopher Richards for his help with editing and transcribing my interview with Philip Zimbardo, and to Eddie Guzelian and Ethan Pines for helping me (over beers and oysters) to come up with a title for the book at the very last minute.

As usual, my wife, Jennifer Sommers, provided invaluable editing advice and had to put up with a lot of ranting and hot-tempered resistance in the process. I don't know how I could have completed the project without her assistance. I dedicate this book to Jen and to my daughter Eliza.

Finally, my deepest gratitude to Frans de Waal, Josh Greene, Jonathan Haidt, Joe Henrich, William Ian Miller, Michael Ruse, Steve Stich, Galen Strawson, Liane Young, and Philip Zimbardo— the distinguished researchers featured in this book. All were exceedingly generous with their time and assistance. Putting together this book has been an education and a pleasure. I hope the reader enjoys it too.

SELECTED READING

FRANS DE WAAL

Chimpanzee Politics, rev. ed. 1998. Baltimore: Johns Hopkins University Press. First published 1982.

Good Natured: The Origins of Right and Wrong in Humans and Other Animals. 1996. Cambridge, MA: Harvard University Press.

Our Inner Ape: A Leading Primatologist Explains Why We Are Who We Are. 2005. New York: Riverhead.

Primates and Philosophers: How Morality Evolved. S. Macedo & J. Ober, eds. 2006. Princeton, NJ: Princeton University Press.

JOSHUA GREENE

The Terrible, Horrible, No Good, Very Bad Truth About Morality and What to Do About It. (Tentative title.) Forthcoming. Penguin.

JONATHAN HAIDT

Flourishing: Positive Psychology and the Life Well-Lived. With C.L.M. Keyes. 2003. Washington DC: American Psychological Association.

The Happiness Hypothesis. 2006. New York: Basic Books.

JOSEPH HENRICH

Foundations of Human Sociality. 2004. New York: Oxford University Press.

Why Humans Cooperate. 2007. New York: Oxford University Press.

WILLIAM IAN MILLER

Humiliation. 1993. Ithaca, NY: Cornell University Press.

The Mystery of Courage. 2000. Cambridge: Harvard University Press.

Faking It. 2003. Cambridge: Cambridge University Press.

Eye for an Eye. 2006. Cambridge: Cambridge University Press.

MICHAEL RUSE

Taking Darwin Seriously: A Naturalistic Approach to Philosophy. 1986. New York: Blackwell.

Can a Darwinian be a Christian? The Relationship Between Science and Religion. 2001. Cambridge: Cambridge University Press.

Darwinism and its Discontents. 2006. Cambridge: Cambridge University Press.

STEPHEN STICH

The Fragmentation of Reason: Preface to a Pragmatic Theory of Cognitive Evaluation. 1990. Cambridge, MA: MIT Press.

Deconstructing the Mind. 1996. New York: Oxford University Press.

Mindreading: An Integrated Account of Pretence, Self-Awareness and Understanding Other Minds. With Shaun Nichols. 2003. New York: Oxford University Press.

GALEN STRAWSON

Freedom and Belief. 1986. Oxford: Clarendon Press.

Mental Reality. 1994. Cambridge, MA: MIT Press.

Real Materialism and Other Essays. 2008. Oxford: Clarendon Press.

Selves: An Essay in Revisionary Metaphysics. 2009. New York: Oxford University Press.

PHILIP ZIMBARDO

The Psychology of Attitude Change and Social Influence. 1991. New York: McGraw-Hill.

The Lucifer Effect: Understanding How Good People Turn Evil. 2007. New York and London: Random House.

The Time Paradox: The New Psychology of Time that Will Change Your Life. 2008. New York: Free Press.

ABOUT THE
AUTHOR

Tamler Sommers is a professor of philosophy at the University of Houston. He is currently writing a book about cross-cultural perspectives on moral responsibility entitled *Relative Justice* (from Princeton University Press).